I0605628

Dear Reader,

When I started my food journey fifteen years ago with my website CavegirlCuisine.com, I began learning about the food I was eating. I came to understand that a calorie isn't just a calorie and there are also macronutrients—carbohydrates, proteins, and fats—at play in all the food choices I make. One important lesson I learned was that there is no need to completely eliminate a food group from my diet. For example, carbohydrates come in many forms—both healthy and unhealthy—and understanding which is which is crucial. Also, protein is an essential building block for the body, but it is critical to consume it in a balanced way **for optimum benefits**. And finally, I learned that eating the right carbohydrates with the right complement of protein and healthy fats can manage and even reverse health issues such as diabetes and heart disease.

I guarantee that when you choose to eat high-protein, low-carbohydrate meals, you will not be giving up flavor. By just tweaking your routine and adding new recipes like the ones in this book, you will **start to notice differences** in how your body reacts. You will sleep better, have clearer skin, enjoy increased energy, and even lose some weight along the way. Don't think of this as a diet. Don't try to be perfect. Just start thinking about eating real food again and go at your own speed.

This cookbook will guide you through **easy-to-make recipes** that will have you and your family wanting more. There are tips along the way and suggestions on how to adapt the recipes to what you have on hand. This is your journey. This is your kitchen. Have fun with these recipes, learn a few tricks, and cheers to your healthy future.

Happy eating,
Michelle Fagone

Welcome to the Everything® Series!

These handy, accessible books give you all you need to tackle a difficult project, gain a new hobby, comprehend a fascinating topic, prepare for an exam, or even brush up on something you learned back in school but have since forgotten.

You can choose to read an Everything® book from cover to cover or just pick out the information you want from our four useful boxes: Questions, Facts, Alerts, and Essentials. We give you everything you need to know on the subject, but throw in a lot of fun stuff along the way too.

question
Answers to common questions.

fact
Important snippets of information.

alert
Urgent warnings.

essential
Quick handy tips.

We now have more than 600 Everything® books in print, spanning such wide-ranging categories as cooking, health, parenting, personal finance, wedding planning, word puzzles, and so much more. When you're done reading them all, you can finally say you know Everything®!

PUBLISHER Karen Cooper

MANAGING EDITOR Lisa Laing

ASSOCIATE COPY DIRECTOR Casey Ebert

PRODUCTION EDITOR Jo-Anne Duhamel

ACQUISITIONS EDITOR Julia Belkas

DEVELOPMENT EDITOR Brett Palana-Shanahan

EVERYTHING® SERIES COVER DESIGNER Erin Alexander

THE EVERYTHING® *Easy* High-Protein, Low-Carb Cookbook

200 Satisfying Recipes to Lose Weight, Build Muscle, and Live a Healthy Lifestyle

Michelle Fagone
With Melinda Boyd, DCN, RD, FAND

ADAMS MEDIA
NEW YORK AMSTERDAM/ANTWERP LONDON TORONTO
SYDNEY/MELBOURNE NEW DELHI

To my friends at the Purrfect Day Cat Café in Louisville, Kentucky:
Thank you for giving me a new "family" away from home and
doing all that you do for the Kentucky fur babies!
Much love, xoxo, Michelle

Adams Media
An Imprint of Simon & Schuster, LLC
100 Technology Center Drive
Stoughton, MA 02072

An Everything® Series Book.

Everything® and everything.com® are registered trademarks of Simon & Schuster, LLC.

First Adams Media trade paperback edition December 2025

ADAMS MEDIA and colophon are registered trademarks of Simon & Schuster, LLC.

Interior design by Colleen Cunningham
Photographs by Emily Weeks

Manufactured in the United States of America

10 9 8 7 6 5 4 3 2 1

Library of Congress Control Number: 2025942655

ISBN 978-1-5072-2511-0
ISBN 978-1-5072-2512-7 (ebook)

Contents

Introduction 11

Chapter 1.
High-Protein, Low-Carb Living 13

Understanding Macronutrients 14

Why Go High-Protein, Low-Carb? 15

Groups Who Can Benefit from a High-Protein, Low-Carb Diet 16

How to Read Food Labels 18

High-Protein, Low-Carb Food Choices and Preparation 19

Your High-Protein, Low-Carb Kitchen 21

Chapter 2.
Breakfast and Brunch 23

Mediterranean Egg Bites 24

Cubano Egg Cups 25

Bacon, Cheddar, and Arugula Frittata 26

Reuben Frittata 27

Ham, Swiss, and Roasted Red Pepper Frittata 28

Classic Breakfast Casserole 30

Creamy Ricotta Chive Scrambled Eggs 31

Cheddar Cheesy Scrambled Eggs 32

Breakfast Sausage Patties 33

Morning Hash Bowls 34

Huevos Rancheros with Salsa Verde 35

Goat Cheese Avocado Toast 37

Breakfast Denver Burritos 38

South-of-the-Border Breakfast Burritos 39

Caprese Avocado Toast 40

Smoked Salmon and Cottage Cheese Toast 41

Cinnamon Berry and Cottage Cheese Toast 42

Loaded Yogurt Bowls 43

Chocolate Banana Protein Smoothie 43

Five-Ingredient Fluffy Pancakes 44

Hard-Boiled Quail Eggs 46

Tropical Protein Smoothie 46

Chapter 3. Appetizers and Dips 47

Curried Deviled Eggs 48
Buffalo Chicken Deviled Eggs 49
Baked Chicken Wings 50
Three-Ingredient Stuffed Mushrooms 51
Fruity Caprese Skewers 53
Caramelized Onion Dip 54
Spinach Tots 55
Buffalo Chicken Dip 56
Blue Cheese Dip 57
Baked Pimento Cheese Jalapeño Poppers 57
Spinach and Crab Dip 58
Mini Cheese Balls 59
Roasted Red Pepper Hummus 61
Onion and Bacon Jam 62
Pimento Cheese 63
Honey Mustard Dipping Sauce 64
Black Bean Hummus 65
Artichoke Heart Hummus 66
Raw Oysters with Cucumber Shallot Relish 67
Chilled Shrimp Cocktail 68
Steak Bites with Blue Cheese Crumbles 70

Chapter 4. Poultry 71

Whole Roasted Chicken 72
Chicken Thighs, Brussels Sprouts, and Pears 73
Chicken Lettuce Wraps 74
Chicken Gyro Bowls 75
Sheet Pan Drumsticks and Vegetables 77
Hasselback Chicken Breasts 78
Chicken Piccata 79
Bruschetta Chicken Tenders 80
Chicken Parmesan 81
Fajita-Style Chicken Kebabs 82
Island Chicken Thighs 84
Chicken Thighs with Creamy Dijon Sauce 85
Creamy Dill Chicken Bites 86
Easy Chicken Casserole 87
Chicken Meatballs with Pesto 89
Sloppy Turkey Janes 90
Enchilada Turkey Pie 91
Spicy Cabbage and Turkey Smoked Sausage 92
Quick Turkey Stir-Fry 94
Marinated Turkey Legs 95
Cornish Hens 96

Chapter 5. Beef, Pork, and Lamb 97

Bunless Beef Sliders 98

Mini Meatloaves 99

Margarita Flank Steak 100

Taco Meatzza 101

Beef and Broccoli 103

Cowboy Sirloin Steaks 104

Sweet Pepper Steak 105

No-Noodle Beef Stroganoff 106

Beef Soft Tacos 107

Philly Cheesesteak Bowls 108

Sloppy Joe Casserole 110

Mozzarella-Stuffed Meatballs 111

Stuffed Beefsteak Tomatoes 112

Oven Pulled Pork 113

Thai Burger Patties with Quick-Pickled Vegetables 115

Pork Egg Roll Bowl 116

Roasted Pork Tenderloin 117

Skillet Pork Chops with Plums 118

Mushroom and Swiss-Stuffed Pork Chops 119

Baked Baby Back Pork Ribs 120

Garlic Basil Frenched Rack of Lamb 122

Lamb Burgers 123

Chapter 6. Fish and Seafood 125

Crusted Chili Lime Cod 126

Baked Fish Sticks 127

Cast Iron Cod and Ratatouille-Style Vegetables 129

Salmon Patties with Sriracha Lime Crema 130

Snow Crab Legs with Chili Mustard Butter 131

Curried Coconut Shrimp 132

Butter Shrimp 133

Parmesan Flounder 133

Pan-Seared Salmon 135

Thai Peanut “Noodles” with Shrimp 136

BBQ Shrimp 137

Sea Bass in Parchment (en Papillote) 138

Baked Tilapia 139

Creamy Hearts of Palm Linguini with Shrimp 140

Pecan-Crusted Barramundi 142

Caper and Lemon Butter Halibut 143

Mexican Mussels 144

Lobster Lettuce Wraps 145

Fish Tacos 147

Steamed Littleneck Clams 148

Steamed Lobster Tails 149

Baked Crab Cakes 150

Chapter 7.
Vegetarian Mains and Sides 151

Loaded Mashed Cauliflower 152
Lower-Carb Garlic Mashed Potatoes 153
Air Fryer Avocado Fries 154
Cast Iron Brussels Sprouts 155
Veggie Sammie 156
Roasted Halloumi and Cauliflower 158
Oven-Roasted Parmesan Broccoli 159
Dilled Roasted Carrots 160
Roasted Radishes 161
Summer Squash Casserole 162
Sweet and Tangy Braised Red Cabbage 163
Zucchini Tacos 165
Baked Onion Rings 166
Bean Burger Patties 167
Tex-Mex Zucchini Boats 168
Protein Lentil Bowls 169
Blistered Tomatoes 170
Grilled Green Tomatoes 171
Portobello Pizzas 172
Quick-Pickled Red Onions 174
Slow Cooker Mushrooms 174

Chapter 8.
Soups, Stews, and Chilis 175

Homemade Chicken Broth 176
Homemade Beef Broth 177
Bacon Cauli Fauxtato Soup 178
Chorizo and Black Bean Soup 179
Creamy Broccoli Soup 181
Wild Mushroom Soup 182
Fire-Roasted Tomato Soup 183
Thai Coconut Chicken Soup 184
Cheeseburger Soup 185
Southern Potlikker Soup 186
Navy Bean Soup 187
Easy French Onion Soup 188
Duck and Butternut Squash Stew 190
Vegetable Soup 191
Carrot and Ginger Miso Soup 192
Quick Miso Soup 193
Tex-Mex Turkey Chili 194
Fish Stew 195
Crab Bisque 197
Manhattan Clam Chowder 198
Cowgirl Cactus Chili 199
Chicken Chili Verde 200
Beef Stew 201

Chapter 9.
Salads, Dressings, Sauces, Salsas 203

Caesar Wedge Salad **204**

Southern Egg Salad **204**

Watermelon Salad **205**

Leftover Rotisserie Chicken Salad **206**

Fennel Salad with Grapefruit Caper Vinaigrette **207**

BELTA Salad **208**

Brussels Sprouts Salad **210**

Cocktail Sauce **210**

Simple Vinaigrette **211**

Kickin' Dijon Mustard Dressing **212**

Creamy Caesar Dressing **213**

Thousand Island Dressing **214**

Homemade Ranch Dressing **215**

Mediterranean Cannellini Bean Salad **217**

Worcestershire Sauce **218**

Russian Dressing **219**

Blueberry Ketchup **220**

Tzatziki Sauce **221**

Cucumber Watermelon Feta Salsa **222**

Basil and Grapefruit Pesto **224**

Jalapeño and Cilantro Pesto **225**

Almond Sage Pesto **226**

Roasted Salsa Verde **227**

Strawberry Basil Salsa **228**

Peach and Sweet Pepper Salsa **228**

Chapter 10.
Snacks and Desserts 229

Pimento Cheese–Stuffed Celery **230**

Piña Colada–Style Protein Popsicles **230**

Spiced Pepitas **231**

BLT Cups **233**

Spicy Lime Tortilla Chips **234**

Sesame Nori Chips **235**

Cinnamon-Spiced Apple Chips **236**

Portable Cherry Parfaits **237**

Grilled Peaches with Whipped Greek Yogurt **238**

Chocolate Almond Butter Fudge **240**

Peanut Butter Fudge **241**

Chocolate Nutty Mixed Clusters **242**

Chocolate Mousse **243**

Prosciutto-Wrapped Cantaloupe **245**

Balsamic Basil Strawberries **246**

Peachy Watermelon Popsicles **246**

Ginger Plums **247**

Peanut and Chocolate–Covered Strawberries **248**

Blueberry Protein Smoothie Bowl **249**

Strawberry Banana Protein Popsicles **250**

Individual Cheesecake Cups **252**

Trail Mix **253**

Pumpkin Pudding **254**

Weekly Meal Plans 255

Index 264

Introduction

Looking to lose weight? Increase your energy levels? Promote muscle growth? Find an overall healthier new you? With *The Everything® Easy High-Protein, Low-Carb Cookbook*, you can find advice, recipes, and meal plans to help you do all these things. This book will show you the powerful benefits of high-protein, low-carb meals and make your health journey both enjoyable and sustainable.

The two hundred recipes in this book will help you make satisfying meals that will keep you feeling full and energized without missing out on flavor! From breakfasts and snacks to dinners and desserts, these easy-to-follow recipes will keep your taste buds happy while supporting your nutrition and health goals. Not only are these recipes easy to make, but they also use common, everyday ingredients so you don't have to spend your valuable time running out to the grocery store. You will find new, healthier versions of your favorite foods that you'll want to make again and again, such as:

- Bacon, Cheddar, and Arugula Frittata
- Buffalo Chicken Dip
- Baked Baby Back Pork Ribs
- Fajita-Style Chicken Kebabs
- Three-Ingredient Stuffed Mushrooms
- Crab Bisque
- Cucumber Watermelon Feta Salsa
- Individual Cheesecake Cups
- And more!

In addition, Chapter 1 will walk you through the high-protein, low-carb diet, showing you how reducing your carb intake and focusing on protein-rich foods can help your body work more efficiently and lead to a sounder sleep schedule, a more efficient metabolism, higher energy levels, and better digestion. You'll discover how to correctly read food labels so you can make the right food choices, and you'll find tips on food preparation and kitchen tools. Plus, as an added bonus, an appendix of meal plans will help take the worry out of meal planning and keep you on track.

Whether you are new to the high-protein, low-carb lifestyle or are just looking for new inspiration, you'll find plenty of delicious recipes and valuable information in this book that will help you take charge of your health journey. It is time to say hello to the power of protein and goodbye to excess carbs!

CHAPTER 1

High-Protein, Low-Carb Living

In a world obsessed with quick weight loss, a lot of dietary trends tend to concentrate on one aspect of weight loss, whether that be eliminating fat, cutting carbs, or eating increased (often outrageous) amounts of protein. The truth is that there are three macronutrients that keep your body going: fats, carbohydrates, and proteins. Any one of the three should not be eliminated from your diet; rather, you should aim for a balanced intake of each. This balance can address multiple health goals simultaneously, such as building muscle, reducing inflammation, and even dealing with the challenges of menopause. This chapter will discuss the basics of the high-protein, low-carb diet; show you some of the ways it can benefit your health; and help prepare you for success.

Understanding Macronutrients

In order to understand the benefits of a high-protein, low-carb diet, it is critical to know exactly what proteins and carbohydrates are and how they affect your body. Macronutrients, or macros, are the primary nutrients your body requires in large amounts to produce energy, support growth, and maintain overall health. The macronutrients are proteins, carbohydrates, and fats. If a diet ever asks you to give up one of those macronutrients completely or reduce your intake far below recommended levels, it is not a healthy choice.

- **Carbohydrates** are your body's preferred and quickest energy source, especially for the brain and muscles during activity. They are found in both simple forms, like table sugar and fruit, and complex forms, like whole grains and vegetables.
- **Proteins** are made up of amino acids, which are the building blocks for muscles, enzymes, hormones, and immune cells. Common protein sources include meat, fish, eggs, dairy, beans, and tofu.
- **Fats** are essential for hormone production, brain function, cell structure, and the absorption of fat-soluble vitamins (A, D, E, and K). Healthy fat sources include avocados, nuts, seeds, olive oil, and fatty fish.

A balanced intake of macronutrients is key to supporting your body's needs. For example, athletes or those trying to build muscle might consume more protein, while someone with a physically demanding job might need more carbohydrates for quick energy. Similarly, a person following a ketogenic or low-carb diet might prioritize fats and protein while keeping carbs very low. Each macro plays a different role, and the right combination can vary widely depending on your goals, age, gender, health conditions, and lifestyle.

For the purposes of this book, we are considering recipes at 25 grams to be high in protein, but your overall diet for the day will ultimately depend on all the foods you choose to consume. It is important that you work with a dietician or medical professional to find out what macronutrient balance is the right one for you and your goals.

fact

The National Academy of Sciences provides specific recommendations, known as AMDRs (Acceptable Macronutrient Distribution Ranges), for all three macros. They are 45–65 percent for carbohydrates, 10–35 percent for proteins, and 20–35 percent for fats. When experts discuss the high versus low of a macronutrient, they are referring to the top versus bottom margins of these ranges.

Understanding macronutrients helps you make better food choices and gives you more control over how your diet impacts your body. Instead of blindly counting calories, consider your three macronutrients when preparing your meals. There are even ways to track your macros if you desire to do so. Whether you want to lose fat, gain muscle, or simply feel more energized, knowing the basics of macros gives you a helpful guide to support your health and fitness journey.

Why Go High-Protein, Low-Carb?

Both the high-protein and low-carb diets have benefits and disadvantages. A high-protein diet focuses on consuming large amounts of the macronutrient protein, while the low-carb diet seeks to prevent the unhealthy overconsumption of carbohydrates, specifically those with added sugars and a lack of fiber. In theory, both these premises are sound, but you should avoid any extreme versions of these diets that entirely cut out a necessary macronutrient. Let's take a look at what each of these diets has to offer.

The High-Protein Diet

A strictly high-protein lifestyle (one in which 30 percent or more of daily calories come from protein) puts emphasis on the consumption of protein-rich foods such as lean meats, fish, eggs, dairy, legumes, and certain plant-based sources like tofu. This dietary approach is often used to support muscle growth, satisfy fullness, and aid in weight management, which is why a lot of athletes and bodybuilders adhere to this lifestyle. Protein plays a crucial role in repairing tissues, producing enzymes and hormones, and maintaining lean body mass, especially during intermittent fasting or concentrated bouts of physical activity. A typical high-protein diet includes about 30 percent of your total daily calories from protein, although this number can vary based on gender, age, activity level, and health goals.

In addition to muscle repair, another key benefit of a high-protein diet is the effect on metabolism and appetite. Protein takes longer to digest than carbohydrates, helping people feel full longer and potentially reducing the urge to overeat. Additionally, protein has a higher thermic effect of food (TEF) than fats or carbs, meaning the body burns more calories digesting protein versus fats or carbohydrates. With that in mind, it is important to choose high-quality protein sources and balance your diet with fiber-rich vegetables, healthy fats, and complex carbohydrates to ensure overall nutritional adequacy and support your long-term health.

The Low-Carb Diet

In today's world, many people assume that *all* carbohydrates are bad, but this couldn't be further from the truth. A low-carb diet focuses on reducing the intake of carbohydrates—primarily found in grains, sugars, fruits, and starchy vegetables—while emphasizing protein and healthy fats as the main sources of energy. The goal is to lower insulin levels and shift the body's metabolism toward burning fat for fuel, which can lead to weight loss and improved metabolic health. Common versions of low-carb diets include the ketogenic (very low-carb, high-fat), Atkins, and Paleo diets, varying in how restrictive their carbohydrate limits are.

Many people follow a low-carb diet to manage conditions such as obesity, type 2 diabetes, and metabolic syndrome, which includes conditions associated with high blood pressure and high blood sugar. Benefits often include improved blood sugar control, lower triglycerides, increased HDL ("good") cholesterol levels, and a reduced appetite due to feeling satiated from eating fats and proteins. And again, it is crucial to ensure your diet is balanced with plenty of non-starchy vegetables and healthy fats like those from avocados, nuts, and olives as well as lean meats and plant-based protein sources. Although there may be some immediate positive results, as with any diet, long-term success depends on variety not only to prevent deficiencies but also to stave off boredom.

essential

Refined grains, such as white bread and most pastas, have been stripped of fiber and nutrients during processing, which can lead to spikes in blood sugar. In contrast, healthy carbohydrates, such as whole grains, fruits, legumes, and vegetables, provide lasting energy, fiber, and essential nutrients. Choosing whole-food sources of carbs supports digestion, heart health, and sustained fullness. Aim to include vegetables with most every meal. Add mushrooms, peppers, and/or onions to your scrambled eggs for a healthy boost to your breakfast; top any dish with a few slices of tomatoes; or steam some fresh broccoli to add as a simple side dish.

The Power of the High-Protein, Low-Carb Diet

Combining both the high-protein and the low-carb diets can achieve a more well-rounded diet than by following either approach on its own. The high-protein intake helps preserve lean muscle mass, supports a more efficient metabolism by increasing calorie burn through TEF, and enhances satiety. This allows you greater long-term success with weight management, making it easier to stick to a reduced-calorie plan without constant hunger. Meanwhile, reducing carbohydrate intake and focusing on healthy carbohydrates can stabilize blood sugar levels and insulin response, encouraging the body to burn that pesky stored fat for energy. This combination promotes fat loss while supporting muscle retention, which is crucial for long-term metabolic health and sustained weight management. Also, a less-strict set of diet rules when following both approaches helps stave off boredom.

Individually, each diet has strengths but also potential downsides if you adhere to only one. A low-carb diet without sufficient protein may lead to muscle loss or decreased energy levels, especially during caloric restriction or fasting windows. Together, they complement each other, managing weaknesses and enhancing strengths. Combining both makes this dietary strategy especially effective for people looking to lose fat, maintain muscle, and improve overall metabolic function.

Groups Who Can Benefit from a High-Protein, Low-Carb Diet

While many people can benefit from a high-protein, low-carb diet, it is especially beneficial for a few groups in particular.

- **People looking to build muscle:** If you are looking to build muscle, you should think twice about consuming large quantities of protein without including healthy carbohydrates. While protein is crucial for muscle growth and repair, carbohydrates supply the energy to train. Without those carbs, your body may even start to break down your existing muscle for energy use. A balanced approach is a much better plan to achieve a stronger body.
- **People on weight loss medications:** The high-protein, low-carb diet is a practical

approach for those looking to lose weight safely without medications as well as for individuals currently using weight loss medications who need to develop healthier eating habits. Protein naturally helps control hunger by keeping you full longer, which helps reduce cravings and supports muscle maintenance. The more lean muscle mass you have, the higher your resting metabolism rate, thereby helping you burn calories at a higher rate even when asleep. Reducing refined carbohydrates helps stabilize blood sugar and insulin levels, which makes a weight loss journey more sustainable. You will be set up for long-term success if you retrain your brain to eat by the principles of this diet.

- **People experiencing inflammation:** For people who are looking to fight inflammation, there are several protein-rich foods that are anti-inflammatory, such as salmon and other fatty fish, nuts, and seeds. In addition, when you follow this diet you also naturally gravitate toward healthier forms of carbohydrates, which means you will be consuming more antioxidant-rich (and inflammation-fighting) foods like fruits and vegetables. By choosing lean cuts of meat and making smarter protein choices, like reducing red meat intake, you will be cutting down on foods (like red meat) that are pro-inflammatory. Additionally, limiting added sugars on this diet will naturally reduce the amount of added sugar consumption, which will cut down on pro-inflammatory food consumption.
- **Perimenopausal and menopausal women:** Women in these stages of life can benefit from this diet because it can help support hormonal balance, alleviate fatigue, and aid in overall metabolic health. During these stages of life, women typically undergo a natural drop in their estrogen levels, which can contribute to elevated insulin resistance, increased abdominal fat, and loss of muscle mass. The higher protein intake can contribute to higher muscle retention. The lower carbohydrate intake can help stabilize blood sugar and insulin levels.
- **Mature adults:** As we age, our bodies naturally lose muscle and our metabolism starts to slow. This inevitably leads to a vicious cycle of weight gain and energy loss. If you have less energy, you are moving less, causing weight gain. If you are gaining weight, your energy level may feel low, leading to decreased activity, and so on. Consuming more protein helps maintain existing muscles, and eating fewer refined carbohydrates can improve insulin levels and reduce health risks. Because protein keeps you full longer, you will also be less likely to snack throughout the day, aiding in maintaining a healthy weight and staying healthy longer.
- **People living with diabetes:** People who have diabetes should prioritize protein intake at meals to help manage blood sugar levels and support overall health. Unlike carbohydrates, protein does not create sharp spikes in blood glucose and can help with satiation, aiding in portion control. The combination of high-protein and low-carb can also assist with weight management and insulin sensitivity, which are both crucial for a person with diabetes.

- **People looking to improve heart health:** For those looking to improve heart health, a high-protein, low-carb approach can be heart-smart when prioritizing the right ingredients. Prioritizing lean proteins like poultry, fish, and plant-based options while limiting red and processed meats helps reduce saturated fat intake. Incorporating omega-3-rich foods like salmon, walnuts, and chia seeds, along with fiber, with an emphasis on soluble fiber from vegetables and beans, can support healthy cholesterol levels and overall cardiovascular function.

How to Read Food Labels

The Nutrition Facts label found on food packaging provides information on the macronutrients—protein, fats, and carbohydrates—contained in foods you buy, as well as other helpful information. However, unless you understand how to read the label, this information may not mean very much to you.

alert

It's important to remember that the percentages on Nutrition Facts labels represent the percent of the daily value (DV) based on a standard 2,000-calorie diet.

Here is some of the information listed on the labels:

- **Serving size:** Labels must identify the size of a serving. The nutritional information listed on a label is based on a single serving. Take note that a package that seems like a single serving may contain more than one serving. Read the label to make sure.
- **Amount per serving:** Each label identifies the quantities of nutrients and food constituents in a single serving (and sometimes the entire package depending on the food). These include the caloric value of the food as well as the amounts of fat, cholesterol, sodium, carbohydrates, fiber, sugars, added sugars, and protein per serving.
- **Percent daily value:** This indicates how much of a specific nutrient a serving contains based on an average 2,000-calorie diet.
- **Ingredients list:** This is a list of the ingredients in descending order of predominance and weight.

Grams of Carbohydrate or Grams of Sugar?

There are several parts to the carbohydrate section of the Nutrition Facts label. Total Carbohydrate represents the full amount of carbohydrate grams found in a food. Beneath the Total Carbohydrate are other listings: Fiber, Sugars, Added Sugars, and sometimes Sugar Alcohols. It is important to know that all of these are part of Total Carbohydrate, though they have differing effects on blood sugar since all carbohydrates are not created equal.

FIBER

Look for foods where the fiber content is a large part of the total carbohydrates. The Dietary Guidelines for Americans recommends a minimum of 14 grams per 1,000 calories, which works out to roughly 25 grams per day for women and

38 grams for men. Foods with 5 grams of fiber per serving provide an excellent source.

SUGARS

Since the updated Nutrition Facts label was introduced, sugars are separated into those naturally occurring and those added to the product. Items such as milk, plain yogurt, fruit, and vegetables have naturally occurring sugar, which is counted under the Sugars total, but not Added Sugars. For example, 1 cup of milk has 12 grams of sugar from the naturally occurring lactose. Those 12 grams will be listed under Sugars, but Added Sugars will be 0.

ADDED SUGARS

Sugars are sometimes added during the processing of foods such as sweetened beverages, cookies, ice cream, cereal, crackers, yogurt, salad dressing, sauces, marinades, and more. These are listed in the ingredients as dextrose, fructose, lactose, table sugar, beet sugar, honey, corn syrup, turbinado, agave, coconut sugar, and more. The American Heart Association recommends limiting added sugars to 25 grams (6 teaspoons) per day for women and 37 grams (9 teaspoons) per day for men.

SUGAR ALCOHOLS

Some foods will also include a Sugar Alcohols listing under Total Carbohydrates. Sugar alcohols are sweeteners that contain anywhere from zero to half the calories of regular sugar. They exist naturally in certain fruits and vegetables, but some are artificial and are included in processed foods to decrease the added sugars. You will likely find sugar alcohols in many foods labeled "sugar free" or "no sugar added." These may include sorbitol, xylitol, mannitol, erythritol, maltitol, isomalt, lactitol, and hydrogenated starch hydrolysates.

A Word about Net Carbs

Some foods, especially processed foods designed to be lower in sugar, may include a Net Carbs listing. The term "net carbs" does not have a legal definition, is not used by the Food and Drug Administration, and is not recognized by the American Diabetes Association. Net carbs are determined by subtracting any fiber or sugar alcohols on the label from the total carbohydrates to calculate the available or digestible carbs in the product. This is assuming that fiber and sugar alcohols are not absorbed or metabolized, but some are partially digested and therefore still provide calories as well as impact blood sugar.

The equation used to calculate net carbs is not entirely accurate because the contribution of fiber and sugar alcohols to the total carbohydrates depends on the types present. The type of fiber or sugar alcohols used is not specified on the Nutrition Facts label; therefore, the effect on blood glucose and potential insulin therapy adjustments cannot be determined properly. The bottom line: Food companies are using the term to market products. That's not necessarily a bad thing, but you must exercise caution if you're using net carbs to make decisions about which or how much of a food to consume.

High-Protein, Low-Carb Food Choices and Preparation

Adjusting to a high-protein, low-carb lifestyle is all about food choices and preparation. Most high-protein, low-carb items are going to be found on the perimeter of most grocery stores. Start in the produce aisle and look for items that are seasonal, as produce in season not only tastes better but also is more nutritionally dense. Next, make your way to the meat and seafood section. Wild-caught seafood is always your best choice. It is not only better nutritionally but also free of the antibiotics and pesticides used in some seafood farming. Choose your milk or milk alternative and then grab some cheese and Greek yogurt.

In general, many of the items in the center aisles of the grocery store are overly processed, but there are exceptions. In those center aisles, minimally processed foods you should purchase include dried beans, canned beans with no added salt, dried whole-wheat pasta, whole-wheat bread, peanut butter (with no added sugar and no other added fats like palm oil), unsweetened apple sauce, dried fruits with no added sugar, and dry roasted nuts. Remember to always review the Nutrition Facts label on the foods you are considering buying.

essential

When using herbs, is fresh or dried better? The answer is both. Fresh herbs are delicious in salads or pesto or as a garnish. Dried herbs are less vibrant but are great in soups and sauces. A little hack is to roll or crush dried herbs between your fingers before adding them to a dish as this helps wake up the herbs by releasing their natural aromatic oils and flavor.

The best strategy to keep your high-protein, low-carb diet on track is preparation. Take one day a week to prep a variety of foods. Having pre-cut and pre-cooked foods on hand may help you resist the urge to order delivery of less-than-healthy food after a long day. Here are some suggestions of types of food to prep for the week. You don't have to try them all, but do try a few until you find your groove.

- Cook a whole chicken and then make broth from the bones. You'll not only have chicken for snacks and salads, but you'll also have broth ready for an easy soup recipe during the week.
- Make a new hummus each week. Chop vegetables so you'll have them on hand for your new creation!
- Cottage cheese is loaded with casein, a slow-digesting protein that helps you stay full longer (be sure to look for low-sodium options). Transfer some cottage cheese into portioned lidded cups for a ready-to-grab snack.
- Chop fruit. Having something like watermelon pre-sliced and prepped for snacking makes it easier for you and your family to make better choices.
- If a banana gets too ripe, peel it and place it in a zip-top bag in the freezer. It will be a great addition to a morning smoothie. Because it is frozen, you do not have to use as many ice cubes and can avoid watering down your smoothie.
- Find at least two new recipes you'd like to try during the week and add any new ingredients to your shopping list.
- Portion your favorite nuts and seeds into zip-top bags.

- Quick-pickle vegetables to use in the week ahead.
- Make a favorite salad and portion it into containers to take to work or enjoy for any meal.
- Prepare egg cups for grab-and-go breakfasts on those busy mornings.

question

Can You Freeze Egg Cups?

Yes! Egg cups are great to make during a prep day when thinking about the week ahead. Try varying them by adding different cheeses and vegetables. Once they're completely cooled, add to a lidded glass container or a zip-top bag and freeze. In the morning, simply wrap in a damp paper towel and microwave 30 seconds.

Your High-Protein, Low-Carb Kitchen

In addition to having the right foods, the right kitchen tools are necessary as well. You do not have to have every gadget, but some are crucial to your success.

- **Air fryer:** Air fryers cook foods quickly and efficiently. If you like crispy foods, air frying will give you the texture of fried foods without the excess oil.
- **Cast iron pan:** Cast iron pans are amazing for searing those high-protein meats. There is a reason these have been used for generations!
- **Chef's knife:** Because you will be cutting a lot of vegetables and meats, having one good knife on hand is essential. A dull knife can be dangerous because you are using more force, which increases the likelihood the blade will slip.
- **Cutting boards:** Two cutting boards are generally recommended, one for meat and the other for everything else. (Some people choose to have a third board for seafood.) This helps avoid cross contamination. There are arguments to be made for wood versus plastic when choosing a type of cutting board. Wood blocks are attractive and easier on your knife's blade. However, plastic boards are great when working with certain raw meats, being easier to clean because they can go directly in the dishwasher for high-heat cleaning to avoid any foodborne illnesses.
- **Food processor:** Mini food processors are great for sauces, pesto, and hummus. They are efficient and can go right in the dishwasher for easy cleanup.
- **Glass storage containers:** Buy these in a variety of sizes. They are better than plastic because there are no chemicals that can leach into your food.
- **Immersion blender:** If you like soups, this kitchen tool is a necessity. Instead of transferring hot soups to a stand blender, this "hand" or "stick" blender can be used directly in your soup pot, leaving little mess and reducing cleanup.
- **Silicone baking mats:** These replace disposable parchment paper, and additional oils aren't required.
- **Spice rack:** Herbs and spices are essential for bringing flavor and aroma into your world and

adding healthy chemical compounds to your diet. These compounds, such as flavonoids, polyphenols, and terpenes, work together to provide a range of health benefits.

- **Spiralizer:** This tool is an inexpensive and easy way to make zoodles, or zucchini noodles, in minutes.

As you can see, following a high-protein, low-carbohydrate program is not a fad. Rather than the fleeting diets of the past, this truly represents a lifestyle approach to eating. Eating foods that balance and complement one another is completely sustainable as it promotes strength, energy, and overall well-being. So, open your mind and give the recipes in this book a try. Whatever your approach, whether you're trying one or two new recipes a week or completely overhauling your pantry, know that you are starting a journey toward better health!

CHAPTER 2

Breakfast and Brunch

Mediterranean Egg Bites 24
Cubano Egg Cups 25
Bacon, Cheddar, and Arugula Frittata 26
Reuben Frittata 27
Ham, Swiss, and Roasted Red Pepper Frittata 28
Classic Breakfast Casserole 30
Creamy Ricotta Chive Scrambled Eggs 31
Cheddar Cheesy Scrambled Eggs 32
Breakfast Sausage Patties 33
Morning Hash Bowls 34
Huevos Rancheros with Salsa Verde 35
Goat Cheese Avocado Toast 37
Breakfast Denver Burritos 38
South-of-the-Border Breakfast Burritos 39
Caprese Avocado Toast 40
Smoked Salmon and Cottage Cheese Toast 41
Cinnamon Berry and Cottage Cheese Toast 42
Loaded Yogurt Bowls 43
Chocolate Banana Protein Smoothie 43
Five-Ingredient Fluffy Pancakes 44
Hard-Boiled Quail Eggs 46
Tropical Protein Smoothie 46

Mediterranean Egg Bites

Serves 12

Per Serving

Calories	60
Fat	4g
Sodium	167mg
Carbohydrates	1g
Fiber	0g
Sugar	0g
Protein	5g

Bacon Has Added Sugar?

Yes, it is true. While bacon itself does not contain sugar, many companies will add sugar to the curing process to act as a preservative or to enhance the flavor. Check your labels to find what works best for your intentions.

Although delicious right out of the oven, these egg bites are great to make on your weekly prep day for a quick grab-and-go breakfast during the week! Packed with protein and low in carbs, they help keep you feeling full and energized without the midmorning crash.

5 large eggs
¼ teaspoon salt
¼ teaspoon ground black pepper
2 tablespoons dried basil
4 slices no-sugar-added bacon, cooked and crumbled
½ cup shredded mozzarella cheese
6 cherry tomatoes, halved

1. Preheat oven to 350°F. Spray a 12-cup mini muffin tin with nonstick butter cooking spray.
2. In a large bowl, whisk together eggs, salt, black pepper, and basil. Fold in bacon and mozzarella cheese.
3. Distribute mixture among prepared muffin cups. Tuck a tomato half into each cup.
4. Bake 8 minutes or until eggs are set and lightly browned. Serve warm.

Cubano Egg Cups

These egg cups are savory, protein-packed bites inspired by the classic Cuban sandwich, featuring eggs mixed with mustard, dill pickle relish, ham, and Swiss cheese. Baked in muffin tins, they're perfect for a quick breakfast or snack, with bold, tangy flavors keeping you full until your next meal.

Serves 6

Per Serving

Calories	267
Fat	16g
Sodium	863mg
Carbohydrates	5g
Fiber	0g
Sugar	1g
Protein	24g

8 large eggs

1⁄4 teaspoon salt

1⁄4 teaspoon ground black pepper

2 tablespoons yellow mustard

1⁄4 cup dill pickle relish

1 1⁄2 cups small-diced cooked ham

1 1⁄2 cups shredded Swiss cheese

1. Preheat oven to 350°F. Spray a 12-cup muffin tin with nonstick butter cooking spray.
2. In a medium bowl, whisk eggs with salt, black pepper, and mustard.
3. Distribute relish, ham, and Swiss cheese among muffin cups. Pour egg mixture into each cup. Bake 22 minutes or until eggs are set. Serve warm.

Bacon, Cheddar, and Arugula Frittata

Serves 6

Per Serving

Calories	271
Fat	19g
Sodium	515mg
Carbohydrates	2g
Fiber	0g
Sugar	1g
Protein	17g

Perfect for breakfast or brunch, this protein-rich savory egg dish is loaded with crispy bacon, sharp Cheddar cheese, and peppery arugula. For an added flavor bonus, toss some extra arugula in a Simple Vinaigrette (Chapter 9) and serve it on the side.

6 large eggs
¼ cup heavy cream
¼ teaspoon salt
¼ teaspoon ground black pepper
¼ teaspoon smoked paprika
1 tablespoon all-purpose flour
1 cup fresh arugula
1½ cups shredded sharp Cheddar cheese
5 slices no-sugar-added bacon, cooked and crumbled

1. Preheat oven to 325°F. Spray a 9-inch pie plate with nonstick butter cooking spray.
2. In a large bowl, whisk together eggs, cream, salt, black pepper, paprika, and flour. Fold in arugula, Cheddar cheese, and bacon. Pour into prepared pie plate.
3. Bake 40 minutes or until middle of eggs is set.
4. Let rest 30 minutes before serving warm.

Reuben Frittata

This dish combines savory corned beef, tangy sauerkraut, and melted Swiss cheese in a fluffy egg base, a nod to the flavors of the traditional Reuben sandwich—without the high-carb bread. A drizzle of Thousand Island dressing adds a creamy finish, and the caraway seeds lend a hint of the rye bread that typically bookends this classic sandwich!

Serves 6

Per Serving

Calories	315
Fat	23g
Sodium	608mg
Carbohydrates	3g
Fiber	1g
Sugar	1g
Protein	19g

6 large eggs

1⁄4 cup heavy cream

1⁄4 teaspoon salt

1⁄4 teaspoon ground black pepper

1 teaspoon caraway seeds

1⁄2 cup drained sauerkraut

1 1⁄2 cups shredded Swiss cheese

3⁄4 cup chopped corned beef

2 tablespoons Thousand Island Dressing (Chapter 9)

1. Preheat oven to 325°F. Spray a 9-inch pie plate with nonstick butter cooking spray.
2. In a large bowl, whisk together eggs, cream, salt, black pepper, and caraway seeds. Fold in sauerkraut, Swiss cheese, and corned beef. Pour into prepared pie plate.
3. Bake 40 minutes or until middle of eggs is set.
4. Let rest 30 minutes before serving warm. Drizzle with Thousand Island Dressing just before serving.

Ham, Swiss, and Roasted Red Pepper Frittata

Serves 6

Per Serving

Calories	239
Fat	16g
Sodium	465mg
Carbohydrates	3g
Fiber	0g
Sugar	1g
Protein	18g

Can't Find a Block of Swiss Cheese?

Sometimes it seems like the only way you can find Swiss cheese is in slices. If this your situation, buy the slices and dice them—they will melt just as well as the shreds. Also, Gruyère cheese is a good substitute for the Swiss.

Basically a crustless quiche, this frittata is a great way to get your protein, from both the eggs and the ham. Serve it with a green salad tossed with a Simple Vinaigrette (Chapter 9) and top it with a dollop of sour cream—or a squeeze of sriracha if you're feeling the heat!

6 large eggs
1⁄4 cup heavy cream
1⁄4 teaspoon salt
1⁄4 teaspoon ground black pepper
1⁄4 teaspoon smoked paprika
1⁄4 cup chopped jarred roasted red peppers, patted dry
1 1⁄2 cups shredded Swiss cheese
3⁄4 cup diced cooked ham

1. Preheat oven to 325°F. Spray a 9-inch pie plate with nonstick butter cooking spray.
2. In a large bowl, whisk together eggs, cream, salt, black pepper, and paprika. Fold in roasted red peppers, Swiss cheese, and ham. Pour mixture into prepared pie plate.
3. Bake 40 minutes or until middle of eggs is set.
4. Let rest 30 minutes before serving warm.

Classic Breakfast Casserole

Serves 6

Per Serving

Calories	697
Fat	54g
Sodium	1,388mg
Carbohydrates	13g
Fiber	7g
Sugar	4g
Protein	36g

Casserole Variations

There are many ways to change up a classic casserole. You can vary the type of cheese, the color of your bell pepper, or the type of meat used. Casseroles are great to make at the end of the week to use up any odds and ends left in your refrigerator.

This casserole combines savory breakfast sausage, sautéed onion and bell pepper, and cubed low-carb bread. The eggs and cream create a smooth custard-like base. This can be made the night before and will certainly be a crowd-pleaser in the morning!

1 tablespoon avocado oil

1 pound ground breakfast sausage

1 medium yellow onion, peeled and diced

1 medium green bell pepper, seeded and diced

4 slices low-carb white bread, cubed

10 large eggs

1¼ cups heavy cream

⅛ teaspoon ground nutmeg

1 teaspoon salt

1 teaspoon ground black pepper

1 (4-ounce) jar pimientos, drained

2 cups shredded Cheddar cheese, divided

1. Preheat oven to 350°F. Spray a 13" × 9" baking dish with nonstick butter cooking spray.
2. Heat oil in a large skillet over medium-high heat. Add sausage, onion, and bell pepper. Cook 6 minutes or until vegetables are tender and sausage is browned. Transfer to a paper towel–lined plate.
3. Add meat mixture to prepared baking dish. Scatter bread cubes over meat.
4. In a large bowl, whisk together eggs, cream, nutmeg, salt, and black pepper. Fold in pimientos and 1 cup cheese. Pour into baking dish and cover with foil. Bake 50 minutes.
5. Remove foil. Scatter remaining cheese over top of casserole and bake an additional 10 minutes or until eggs are set. Let cool 15 minutes. Serve warm.

Creamy Ricotta Chive Scrambled Eggs

If you've never tried ricotta blended into your scrambled eggs, then you are missing out! Not only does ricotta add extra protein to your eggs, but the creaminess is the dreamiest! Ricotta cheese is rich in whey protein, which is easily digestible and supports muscle repair and maintenance.

Serves 4

Per Serving

Calories	248
Fat	18g
Sodium	314mg
Carbohydrates	2g
Fiber	0g
Sugar	1g
Protein	16g

8 large eggs

½ cup ricotta cheese

¼ teaspoon salt

¼ teaspoon ground black pepper

2 tablespoons unsalted butter

¼ cup chopped chives

1. In a medium bowl, add eggs, ricotta cheese, salt, and black pepper. Whisk vigorously.
2. Heat butter in a large skillet over medium heat. Pour in egg mixture. Slowly push mixture around skillet until eggs are set. Do not cook until eggs are dry; they should still be "wet" or glistening.
3. Transfer to plates, garnish with chives, and serve warm.

Cheddar Cheesy Scrambled Eggs

Serves 4

Per Serving

Calories	255
Fat	18g
Sodium	381mg
Carbohydrates	1g
Fiber	0g
Sugar	1g
Protein	16g

These fluffy, buttery scrambled eggs are cooked low and slow, then folded with melted sharp Cheddar cheese for a rich, creamy meal. This protein-packed breakfast is simple and comforting for any morning!

8 large eggs

2 tablespoons whole milk

2 tablespoons unsalted butter

½ cup shredded sharp Cheddar cheese

¼ teaspoon salt

¼ teaspoon ground black pepper

1. In a medium bowl, vigorously combine eggs and whole milk until frothy.
2. Heat butter in a large skillet over medium-low heat. Pour in eggs. Slowly push eggs around skillet until set. Do not cook until dry; eggs should still be "wet" or glistening. Add cheese, salt, and black pepper. Fold eggs several times until cheese is melted.
3. Transfer to plates and serve warm.

Breakfast Sausage Patties

A lot of pre-cooked and pre-packaged breakfast sausages contain sugars and preservatives. But making your own is so easy! You may even want to double or triple this recipe to place in the freezer for future morning meals.

Serves 6

Per Serving

Calories	178
Fat	11g
Sodium	142mg
Carbohydrates	3g
Fiber	0g
Sugar	2g
Protein	14g

1 pound ground pork

3 cloves garlic, peeled and minced

1 tablespoon chopped fresh sage leaves

1 teaspoon fresh thyme leaves

1⁄4 teaspoon red pepper flakes

1⁄4 teaspoon salt

1⁄8 teaspoon ground black pepper

1 tablespoon pure maple syrup

1 tablespoon avocado oil

1. In a large bowl, combine all ingredients except oil. Form mixture into twelve equal patties.
2. Heat oil in a large skillet over medium heat 1 minute. Add sausage patties. Cook until browned, approximately 3 minutes per side.
3. Serve warm.

Morning Hash Bowls

Serves 6

Per Serving

Calories	357
Fat	24g
Sodium	332mg
Carbohydrates	7g
Fiber	2g
Sugar	1g
Protein	23g

This recipe might not be the lowest-carb breakfast; however, a sweet potato has a lower glycemic index than your basic russet potato, meaning it causes a slower, steadier rise in blood sugar. Should you eat this every day? No. Is it a better alternative to traditional hash when you have a craving? Yes.

1 tablespoon avocado oil

1 pound ground pork sausage

1 large sweet potato, peeled and grated

1 medium bunch green onions, sliced (white and green parts separated)

1 tablespoon dried Italian seasoning

2 tablespoons unsalted butter

6 large eggs

1 large avocado, peeled, pitted, and sliced

½ teaspoon salt

½ teaspoon ground black pepper

1. Heat oil in a large skillet over medium heat 1 minute. Add sausage, sweet potato, and whites of green onions. Sauté 5 minutes. Add Italian seasoning and stir. Set aside.
2. In a different large skillet, melt butter over medium heat 1 minute. Add eggs and fry to preferred doneness.
3. Divide sausage mixture among individual serving bowls. Top each with a fried egg and avocado slices. Season with salt and black pepper, garnish with greens of green onions, and serve warm.

Huevos Rancheros with Salsa Verde

This high-protein breakfast is a flavor explosion *and* a satisfying way to fuel your morning without a blood sugar crash. Top with a dollop of plain Greek yogurt, sprinkling of fresh cilantro, or drizzle of sriracha for an added indulgence.

Serves 4

Per Serving

Calories	483
Fat	28g
Sodium	1,735mg
Carbohydrates	46g
Fiber	23g
Sugar	7g
Protein	21g

1 (16-ounce) can refried black beans

½ teaspoon ground cumin

½ teaspoon smoked paprika

2 tablespoons unsalted butter

4 large eggs

½ cup shredded Mexican cheese blend

1 teaspoon salt, divided

1 teaspoon ground black pepper, divided

2 large tomatoes, diced

4 (8-inch) low-carb flour tortillas

1 cup Roasted Salsa Verde (Chapter 9)

1 large avocado, peeled, pitted, and diced

1. In a small saucepan, stir together beans, cumin, and paprika. Cover and heat over medium heat 5 minutes or until warmed through. Stir halfway through cooking time.
2. While beans are cooking, melt butter in a large skillet over medium heat. Crack eggs into each quarter of the skillet. Scatter cheese around eggs. Season with ½ teaspoon salt and ½ teaspoon black pepper. Cover and cook 3 minutes or until whites of eggs are opaque and cheese is melted. Remove from heat but keep covered.
3. Place tomatoes in a small bowl. Add remaining salt and black pepper and toss to combine.
4. Place a tortilla on each of four plates. Spread refried beans over each tortilla. Add eggs and cheese. Top with salsa, avocado, and tomatoes. Serve.

Give Those Tomatoes Some Flavor

Do you ever wonder why the fresh tomatoes in restaurants taste better than at home? Salt and pepper are the secret. After dicing or slicing your tomatoes, season them immediately and give them a quick toss *before* adding them to your salad or eggs or serving them as a side.

Goat Cheese Avocado Toast

Here, the funkiness of the goat cheese marries so beautifully with the creaminess of the avocado and the freshness of the tomato. It is a match made in heaven! This low-carb breakfast will help keep you feeling full all morning long with the healthy fats from the avocado and the protein from the goat cheese.

Serves 4

Per Serving

Calories	205
Fat	14g
Sodium	893mg
Carbohydrates	16g
Fiber	12g
Sugar	1g
Protein	13g

1 large ripe avocado, peeled, pitted, and diced
2 cloves garlic, peeled and minced
2 teaspoons lime juice
½ teaspoon salt
4 slices low-carb white bread
1 large beefsteak tomato, cut into 4 slices
½ teaspoon salt
¼ teaspoon ground black pepper
1 cup crumbled goat cheese

1. Preheat broiler on high 5 minutes. Line a baking sheet with parchment paper.
2. In a small bowl, mash together avocado, garlic, lime juice, and salt. Spread over bread slices. Place bread slices on baking sheet.
3. Season tomato slices with salt and black pepper. Add a slice to each piece of bread.
4. Distribute goat cheese over tomatoes.
5. Broil bread 3 minutes or until goat cheese is melty and slightly browned. Serve warm.

Change Up Your Bread!

There are several brands and flavors of low-carb, pre-sliced bread. Find what suits your needs and taste buds, whether that's a certain brand or plain, seeded, or Hawaiian-style.

Breakfast Denver Burritos

Serves 4

Per Serving

Calories	446
Fat	27g
Sodium	2,076mg
Carbohydrates	18g
Fiber	11g
Sugar	2g
Protein	34g

The Colors of the Bell Pepper Rainbow

Bell peppers have different flavor profiles according to their color. Green bell peppers are unripened and have a slightly more bitter taste. Red peppers are the sweetest but lack the crunch of the others. Orange peppers are more fruity and yellow ones are mild. Try them all, as they all lend different nutrients to your diet.

This recipe gives you all the flavors of a traditional Denver omelet but condensed into a burrito for an easy grab-and-go breakfast. This low-carb, high-protein option keeps you energized without the heaviness of a traditional wrap. Perfect for busy mornings when you need a quick, nutritious start.

6 large eggs
1 teaspoon salt
1 teaspoon ground black pepper
2 tablespoons salted butter
1 medium white onion, peeled and diced
1 medium green bell pepper, seeded and diced
2 cups diced cooked ham
1 cup shredded Cheddar cheese
4 (8-inch) low-carb flour tortillas

1. In a small bowl, whisk together eggs, salt, and black pepper.
2. In a large skillet, heat butter over medium heat 1 minute or until butter is melted. Add onion, bell pepper, and ham. Sauté 3 minutes or until onion and bell pepper are tender.
3. Add eggs to skillet and scramble 2–4 minutes until eggs are scrambled but not dry. Top eggs with cheese. Cover skillet and remove from heat 3 minutes.
4. Place a tortilla on each of four plates. Distribute egg mixture on center of each tortilla. Roll up tortilla and fold in the sides. Serve warm.

South-of-the-Border Breakfast Burritos

These breakfast burritos are packed with proteins like scrambled eggs, spicy chorizo, and cotija cheese, all wrapped up in a low-carb tortilla. A topping of fresh salsa and creamy sour cream adds a fresh, cooling kick to start the day right. If you don't have cotija cheese, you can use shredded Mexican cheese blend instead.

Serves 4

Per Serving

Calories	462
Fat	32g
Sodium	2,116mg
Carbohydrates	23g
Fiber	13g
Sugar	6g
Protein	24g

6 large eggs

1 teaspoon salt

1 teaspoon ground black pepper

2 tablespoons unsalted butter

¼ pound ground chorizo

1 medium white onion, peeled and diced

1 medium poblano pepper, seeded and diced

1 cup crumbled cotija cheese

4 (8-inch) low-carb flour tortillas

1 cup salsa

4 tablespoons sour cream

¼ cup chopped fresh cilantro

1. In a small bowl, whisk together eggs, salt, and black pepper.
2. In a large skillet, add butter and heat over medium heat 1 minute until butter is melted. Add chorizo, onion, and poblano pepper. Sauté 3 minutes until onion and pepper are tender and chorizo is cooked through.
3. Add eggs to skillet and scramble 2–4 minutes until eggs are scrambled but not dry. Top eggs with cheese. Cover skillet and remove from heat 3 minutes.
4. Place a tortilla on each of four plates. Distribute egg mixture on center of each tortilla. Roll up tortilla and fold in the sides. Garnish with salsa, sour cream, and cilantro. Serve warm.

Caprese Avocado Toast

Serves 4

Per Serving

Calories	180
Fat	9g
Sodium	922mg
Carbohydrates	21g
Fiber	12g
Sugar	5g
Protein	12g

Additions and Substitutions

If you want to use a fresh ball of mozzarella cheese instead of the shredded variety, just thinly slice it before adding it to your toast. And if you want to garnish the final product with just a little olive oil, go for it, as it is such a healthy oil to add to your diet.

Avocado toast does not have to be boring. Add a little Mediterranean flair to your brunch with this caprese variation—fresh basil is the key ingredient for bringing the dish to life. The low-carb bread helps keep this delicious breakfast within reasonable carb limits.

1 large ripe avocado, peeled, pitted, and diced

2 cloves garlic, peeled and minced

2 teaspoons lime juice

½ teaspoon salt

4 slices low-carb white bread

1 large beefsteak tomato, cut into 4 slices

½ teaspoon salt

¼ teaspoon ground black pepper

1 cup shredded mozzarella cheese

6 fresh basil leaves, sliced

1 tablespoon balsamic vinegar reduction

1. Preheat broiler on high 5 minutes.
2. In a small bowl, mash together avocado, garlic, lime juice, and salt. Spread over the bread.
3. Season both sides of tomato slices with salt and black pepper. Add a slice to each piece of bread.
4. Distribute mozzarella cheese over tomatoes.
5. Broil 3 minutes or until cheese is melty and slightly browned. Garnish with basil and a drizzle of vinegar reduction. Serve.

Smoked Salmon and Cottage Cheese Toast

Who needs bagels for a deli-tastic meal? Everything Bagel Seasoning will give you that familiar nod that your taste buds have been missing. And with about 11 grams of protein per serving, cottage cheese packs a protein punch in this dish.

Serves 2

Per Serving

Calories	170
Fat	4g
Sodium	1,228mg
Carbohydrates	17g
Fiber	10g
Sugar	4g
Protein	21g

1⁄3 cup cottage cheese
1 teaspoon Everything Bagel Seasoning
2 slices keto soft white bread, toasted
2 medium Roma tomatoes, sliced
1⁄4 teaspoon salt
1⁄4 teaspoon ground black pepper
4 ounces smoked salmon
1⁄4 large red onion, peeled and thinly sliced
2 teaspoons capers, drained

1. In a small bowl, combine cottage cheese and Everything Bagel Seasoning. Spread on toast.
2. Season both sides of tomato slices with salt and black pepper. Add tomatoes to each slice of toast. Distribute salmon over tomato slices.
3. Garnish with red onion slices and capers. Serve.

Differences in Smoked Salmon

If you are confused about which smoked salmon to buy, it is always better to choose the "wild-caught" variety. Because of the fish's diet, not only will the color be richer but the flavor will be deeper and more intense too.

Cinnamon Berry and Cottage Cheese Toast

Serves 2

Per Serving

Calories	94
Fat	2g
Sodium	471mg
Carbohydrates	17g
Fiber	10g
Sugar	5g
Protein	10g

Fresh Lemon Juice versus Store-Bought

With most things, fresh is always the best option. However, keep one of those store-bought bottles of lemon juice in your refrigerator when you need just a squeeze here or there, like on fresh fruit, fish, or chicken. This is a convenient grab-and-go item and more cost-effective for small jobs.

Although blueberries are the go-to in this recipe, don't be afraid to try strawberries, peaches, cherries, or whatever is in season and strikes your fancy! The cottage cheese in this dish helps give the recipe a protein boost.

½ cup blueberries
⅛ teaspoon salt
½ teaspoon lemon juice
¼ teaspoon ground cinnamon
¼ teaspoon vanilla extract
⅓ cup cottage cheese
2 slices keto soft white bread, toasted

1. In a small bowl, combine blueberries, salt, lemon juice, cinnamon, and vanilla extract. Refrigerate blueberries in marinade while preparing toast, about 5 minutes.
2. Spread cottage cheese on toasted bread slices.
3. Top with marinated blueberries. Serve.

Loaded Yogurt Bowls

Serves 2	
Per Serving	
Calories	584
Fat	35g
Sodium	234mg
Carbohydrates	43g
Fiber	13g
Sugar	17g
Protein	33g

Whether you use flavored yogurt, different types of fruits or berries, or no-sugar-added granola, or substitute cashew butter for almond butter (or even make your own!), this is a protein-filled bowl of goodness to start your day with a little sweetness.

2 cups plain full-fat Greek yogurt

1 cup diced strawberries

½ cup blackberries

2 tablespoons cashew butter

1 tablespoon ground flax seeds

1 cup no-sugar-added granola

Divide yogurt between individual serving bowls. Top with remaining ingredients. Serve cold.

Chocolate Banana Protein Smoothie

Serves 2	
Per Serving	
Calories	199
Fat	4g
Sodium	340mg
Carbohydrates	17g
Fiber	3g
Sugar	8g
Protein	28g

This protein smoothie is a creamy, satisfying drink that's perfect for breakfast or post-workout fueling. If you are looking to bump up the protein of this smoothie even more, use soy milk in place of the almond milk. This drink is packed with nutrients and is a delicious way to energize your day while supporting muscle recovery.

¼ cup no-sugar-added chocolate protein powder

2 cups unsweetened chocolate almond milk

1 small ripe banana

1 tablespoon honey

½ teaspoon vanilla extract

8 ice cubes

Place all ingredients in a blender and blend until smooth. Pour into two glasses and serve.

Five-Ingredient Fluffy Pancakes

Serves 2

Per Serving

Calories	217
Fat	16g
Sodium	578mg
Carbohydrates	4g
Fiber	0g
Sugar	2g
Protein	12g

Fancy Pancakes!

Consider this recipe your pancake base. You can change up the flavor of your protein powder and even your yogurt to create a different masterpiece every weekend! A dash of cinnamon or some fresh lemon zest would work too.

If you've been missing pancakes on your low-carb diet, this is an easy way to fill that void without going down the carb rabbit hole. Try topping these pancakes with fresh fruit, sugar-free jam, a dollop of yogurt, or even sugar-free maple syrup.

2 large eggs, whisked

½ cup low-fat vanilla Greek yogurt

½ cup no-sugar-added vanilla protein powder

2 teaspoons baking powder

2 tablespoons unsalted butter

1. In a medium bowl, combine eggs, yogurt, protein powder, and baking powder until a smooth batter forms.
2. In a large skillet over medium-high heat, melt butter. Add batter to form four pancakes. Cook 1–2 minutes until browned and then flip. Cook 1 additional minute on the opposite side.
3. Transfer to a serving plate and serve warm.

Hard-Boiled Quail Eggs

Serves 5

Per Serving

Calories	28
Fat	2g
Sodium	25mg
Carbohydrates	0g
Fiber	0g
Sugar	0g
Protein	2g

Upscale grocers and local Asian grocers always have quail eggs on hand. They are cute, have a very peelable shell, take no time to prepare, and can be consumed just like chicken eggs. Containing all nine essential amino acids, eggs are considered a complete protein.

10 quail eggs

1 teaspoon white vinegar

1. Add eggs to a small saucepan and enough water to cover eggs. Add white vinegar.
2. Bring to a boil, then reduce to a rolling boil over medium heat 3 minutes. Transfer immediately to an ice bath to stop the cooking process.
3. Let cool, peel, and serve.

Tropical Protein Smoothie

Serves 2

Per Serving

Calories	260
Fat	4g
Sodium	276mg
Carbohydrates	33g
Fiber	2g
Sugar	23g
Protein	26g

This protein smoothie is a refreshing blend of pineapple, banana, and coconut milk boosted with protein powder for a nourishing, energizing drink. Bursting with bright, tropical island–inspired flavors, it's perfect for breakfast or a post-workout pick-me-up.

¼ cup no-sugar-added vanilla protein powder

2 cups unsweetened Coconutmilk

1 tablespoon honey

1 small ripe banana

1 cup diced pineapple

½ teaspoon rum extract

8 ice cubes

Place all ingredients in a blender and blend until smooth. Pour into two glasses and serve.

CHAPTER 3

Appetizers and Dips

Curried Deviled Eggs 48
Buffalo Chicken Deviled Eggs 49
Baked Chicken Wings 50
Three-Ingredient Stuffed Mushrooms 51
Fruity Caprese Skewers 53
Caramelized Onion Dip 54
Spinach Tots 55
Buffalo Chicken Dip 56
Blue Cheese Dip 57
Baked Pimento Cheese Jalapeño Poppers 57
Spinach and Crab Dip 58
Mini Cheese Balls 59
Roasted Red Pepper Hummus 61
Onion and Bacon Jam 62
Pimento Cheese 63
Honey Mustard Dipping Sauce 64
Black Bean Hummus 65
Artichoke Heart Hummus 66
Raw Oysters with Cucumber Shallot Relish 67
Chilled Shrimp Cocktail 68
Steak Bites with Blue Cheese Crumbles 70

Curried Deviled Eggs

Serves 12

Per Serving

Calories	71
Fat	6g
Sodium	116mg
Carbohydrates	1g
Fiber	0g
Sugar	0g
Protein	3g

Naturally low in carbs and packed with protein, this recipe is a spiced-up twist on the classic, combining creamy yolks with mayonnaise, yellow mustard, and a hint of curry powder for a warm and distinct flavor. Topped with a sprinkle of paprika, these eggs are an eye-catching and flavorful appetizer or snack.

6 large hard-boiled eggs, peeled

¼ cup mayonnaise

½ teaspoon yellow mustard

1 teaspoon dill pickle juice

2 teaspoons curry powder

¼ teaspoon salt

¼ teaspoon ground black pepper

½ teaspoon smoked paprika

1. Cut eggs in half lengthwise. Add yolks to a medium bowl. Set egg whites aside on a medium serving dish.
2. To egg yolks, add mayonnaise, mustard, dill pickle juice, curry powder, salt, and black pepper. Mash together until smooth.
3. Distribute mixture among egg white centers with a spoon or pastry tip.
4. Garnish eggs with a sprinkle of paprika. Serve immediately or chilled.

Buffalo Chicken Deviled Eggs

These deviled eggs are a perfect snack or party appetizer for those following a low-carb, high-protein lifestyle. Each bite delivers satisfying heat and creamy richness without the guilt.

Serves 12	
Per Serving	
Calories	51
Fat	3g
Sodium	83mg
Carbohydrates	0g
Fiber	0g
Sugar	0g
Protein	5g

6 large hard-boiled eggs, peeled and halved lengthwise

¼ cup mayonnaise

1 tablespoon blue cheese crumbles

1 tablespoon buffalo wing sauce

2 tablespoons minced celery

½ cup diced chicken

12 celery leaves

1. Add egg yolks to a medium bowl. Set egg whites aside on a medium serving dish.
2. Add mayonnaise, blue cheese, and buffalo wing sauce. Mash together until smooth. Fold in celery.
3. Distribute mixture among egg white centers with a spoon. Top each with a piece of chicken and a celery leaf. Serve immediately or chilled.

Carbohydrates	8g
Fiber	1g
Sugar	5g
Protein	16g

1 pound baby bella whole mushrooms, stems removed

1 (5.3-ounce) container Boursin Caramelized Onion & Herbs Cheese

¾ pound ground mild Italian sausage

1. Preheat oven to 350°F.
2. Add mushrooms to a large ungreased baking dish. Spray mushrooms with nonstick olive oil spray.
3. Place Boursin cheese in a medium bowl. Set aside.
4. In a medium skillet over medium-high heat, add sausage. Using a wooden spoon, cut and cook sausage 4 minutes or until browned. Add to cheese. Stir until combined.
5. Spoon mixture in mushroom caps. Bake 30 minutes. Transfer stuffed mushrooms to a serving plate and serve warm.

Flavor and Texture Additions

Boursin cheese comes in a variety of flavors that you can use in this recipe to change up the taste. Additionally, Italian sausage comes in a spicy variety if heat is your thing. You can also top each stuffed mushroom cap with crushed pork rinds before baking to add texture.

Baked Chicken Wings

Serves 2

Per Serving

Calories	607
Fat	43g
Sodium	1,098mg
Carbohydrates	5g
Fiber	0g
Sugar	0g
Protein	44g

All I Can Find Are Big Wings!

Sometimes grocery stores will not separate chicken wings into flats and drumettes. They will sell the entire wing, which consists of the drumette, wingette (or flat), and wing tip. Each section is easily separable with a knife. Although the wing tip doesn't lend itself to a tasty snack, save these little gems, as they are perfect when making homemade chicken stock.

Ideal for game day, parties, or a simple weeknight dinner, these baked wings are seasoned to perfection and baked until golden and crispy. Naturally low in carbs and high in protein, they can be served with your favorite dipping sauce without derailing your dietary goals.

12 chicken wings, flats and drumettes
2 tablespoons avocado oil
2 tablespoons coconut aminos
1 teaspoon cayenne pepper
1 teaspoon garlic powder
1 teaspoon dried Italian seasoning
½ teaspoon salt
¼ teaspoon ground black pepper

1. Line a baking sheet with parchment paper.
2. Dry chicken wings with paper towels and set aside. (This will ensure a crisper bake.)
3. In a small bowl, whisk together remaining ingredients. Add wings to bowl and toss to coat. Refrigerate 30 minutes.
4. Preheat oven to 400°F.
5. Place wings on baking sheet. Bake 30 minutes. Flip wings and bake an additional 5 minutes.
6. Place under the broiler on high 2 minutes. Remove from oven and let rest 7 minutes. Serve warm.

Fruity Caprese Skewers

These skewers are a fresh twist on the classic caprese, layering sweet watermelon and peaches with mozzarella balls, basil leaves, and a drizzle of balsamic vinegar. These colorful, bite-sized appetizers are perfect for summer gatherings and offer a balance of sweet, savory, and tangy flavors. You will need eight wooden skewers for this recipe.

Serves 4

Per Serving

Calories	324
Fat	17g
Sodium	532mg
Carbohydrates	28g
Fiber	2g
Sugar	22g
Protein	15g

1 (8-ounce) container fresh ciliegine (mozzarella balls), drained

½ small seedless watermelon, cubed

3 firm medium peaches, peeled, pitted, and cubed

1 small bunch fresh basil leaves

1 small bunch fresh mint leaves

2 tablespoons olive oil

2 tablespoons aged balsamic vinegar

¼ teaspoon salt

¼ teaspoon ground black pepper

1. Skewer ciliegine, watermelon cubes, peach cubes, basil leaves, and mint leaves on each of eight wooden skewers, alternating ingredients.
2. Place skewers in a container large enough to hold them and drizzle them with oil and vinegar. Sprinkle with salt and black pepper. Refrigerate, covered, 30 minutes. Flip skewers and refrigerate another 30 minutes. Serve chilled.

Add Some Protein

If you are looking for an addition of protein (or saltiness), and to achieve another layer of flavor and nutrition, add slices of prosciutto to the skewers.

Caramelized Onion Dip

Yields 2½ cups

Per Serving (Serving size: ¼ cup)

Calories	161
Fat	15g
Sodium	201mg
Carbohydrates	3g
Fiber	0g
Sugar	2g
Protein	2g

You can never go wrong with onion dip—it is loved by all! Great for parties or potlucks, serve this variation with vegetables for dipping to fulfill your onion dip craving but reduce your carb intake.

2 tablespoons avocado oil

1 large yellow onion, peeled and diced (about 2 cups)

½ teaspoon salt

½ cup plain full-fat Greek yogurt

½ cup mayonnaise

1 cup sour cream

1 teaspoon dried dill

½ teaspoon garlic powder

¼ teaspoon cayenne pepper

1. Heat oil in a large skillet over medium-high heat. Add onion and salt. Stir-fry 20 minutes or until browned and starting to caramelize. Remove from heat to cool.
2. In a large bowl, whisk together remaining ingredients. Fold in onion.
3. Refrigerate until ready to serve.

Buffalo Chicken Deviled Eggs

These deviled eggs are a perfect snack or party appetizer for those following a low-carb, high-protein lifestyle. Each bite delivers satisfying heat and creamy richness without the guilt.

Serves 12	
Per Serving	
Calories	51
Fat	3g
Sodium	83mg
Carbohydrates	0g
Fiber	0g
Sugar	0g
Protein	5g

6 large hard-boiled eggs, peeled and halved lengthwise

¼ cup mayonnaise

1 tablespoon blue cheese crumbles

1 tablespoon buffalo wing sauce

2 tablespoons minced celery

½ cup diced chicken

12 celery leaves

1. Add egg yolks to a medium bowl. Set egg whites aside on a medium serving dish.
2. Add mayonnaise, blue cheese, and buffalo wing sauce. Mash together until smooth. Fold in celery.
3. Distribute mixture among egg white centers with a spoon. Top each with a piece of chicken and a celery leaf. Serve immediately or chilled.

Baked Chicken Wings

Serves 2

Per Serving

Calories	607
Fat	43g
Sodium	1,098mg
Carbohydrates	5g
Fiber	0g
Sugar	0g
Protein	44g

All I Can Find Are Big Wings!

Sometimes grocery stores will not separate chicken wings into flats and drumettes. They will sell the entire wing, which consists of the drumette, wingette (or flat), and wing tip. Each section is easily separable with a knife. Although the wing tip doesn't lend itself to a tasty snack, save these little gems, as they are perfect when making homemade chicken stock.

Ideal for game day, parties, or a simple weeknight dinner, these baked wings are seasoned to perfection and baked until golden and crispy. Naturally low in carbs and high in protein, they can be served with your favorite dipping sauce without derailing your dietary goals.

12 chicken wings, flats and drumettes

2 tablespoons avocado oil

2 tablespoons coconut aminos

1 teaspoon cayenne pepper

1 teaspoon garlic powder

1 teaspoon dried Italian seasoning

½ teaspoon salt

¼ teaspoon ground black pepper

1. Line a baking sheet with parchment paper.
2. Dry chicken wings with paper towels and set aside. (This will ensure a crisper bake.)
3. In a small bowl, whisk together remaining ingredients. Add wings to bowl and toss to coat. Refrigerate 30 minutes.
4. Preheat oven to 400°F.
5. Place wings on baking sheet. Bake 30 minutes. Flip wings and bake an additional 5 minutes.
6. Place under the broiler on high 2 minutes. Remove from oven and let rest 7 minutes. Serve warm.

Three-Ingredient Stuffed Mushrooms

These stuffed mushrooms are a low-carb, high-protein delight packed with savory sausage and creamy, flavorful Boursin cheese. Perfect as a satisfying snack or appetizer, they come together quickly with minimal prep and maximum taste.

1 pound baby bella whole mushrooms, stems removed

1 (5.3-ounce) container Boursin Caramelized Onion & Herbs Cheese

3/4 pound ground mild Italian sausage

1. Preheat oven to 350°F.
2. Add mushrooms to a large ungreased baking dish. Spray mushrooms with nonstick olive oil spray.
3. Place Boursin cheese in a medium bowl. Set aside.
4. In a medium skillet over medium-high heat, add sausage. Using a wooden spoon, cut and cook sausage 4 minutes or until browned. Add to cheese. Stir until combined.
5. Spoon mixture in mushroom caps. Bake 30 minutes. Transfer stuffed mushrooms to a serving plate and serve warm.

Serves 4

Per Serving

Calories	477
Fat	40g
Sodium	829mg
Carbohydrates	8g
Fiber	1g
Sugar	5g
Protein	16g

Flavor and Texture Additions

Boursin cheese comes in a variety of flavors that you can use in this recipe to change up the taste. Additionally, Italian sausage comes in a spicy variety if heat is your thing. You can also top each stuffed mushroom cap with crushed pork rinds before baking to add texture.

Fruity Caprese Skewers

These skewers are a fresh twist on the classic caprese, layering sweet watermelon and peaches with mozzarella balls, basil leaves, and a drizzle of balsamic vinegar. These colorful, bite-sized appetizers are perfect for summer gatherings and offer a balance of sweet, savory, and tangy flavors. You will need eight wooden skewers for this recipe.

Serves 4

Per Serving

Calories	324
Fat	17g
Sodium	532mg
Carbohydrates	28g
Fiber	2g
Sugar	22g
Protein	15g

1 (8-ounce) container fresh ciliegine (mozzarella balls), drained

½ small seedless watermelon, cubed

3 firm medium peaches, peeled, pitted, and cubed

1 small bunch fresh basil leaves

1 small bunch fresh mint leaves

2 tablespoons olive oil

2 tablespoons aged balsamic vinegar

¼ teaspoon salt

¼ teaspoon ground black pepper

1. Skewer ciliegine, watermelon cubes, peach cubes, basil leaves, and mint leaves on each of eight wooden skewers, alternating ingredients.
2. Place skewers in a container large enough to hold them and drizzle them with oil and vinegar. Sprinkle with salt and black pepper. Refrigerate, covered, 30 minutes. Flip skewers and refrigerate another 30 minutes. Serve chilled.

Add Some Protein

If you are looking for an addition of protein (or saltiness), and to achieve another layer of flavor and nutrition, add slices of prosciutto to the skewers.

Caramelized Onion Dip

Yields 2½ cups

Per Serving (Serving size: ¼ cup)

Calories	161
Fat	15g
Sodium	201mg
Carbohydrates	3g
Fiber	0g
Sugar	2g
Protein	2g

You can never go wrong with onion dip—it is loved by all! Great for parties or potlucks, serve this variation with vegetables for dipping to fulfill your onion dip craving but reduce your carb intake.

2 tablespoons avocado oil

1 large yellow onion, peeled and diced (about 2 cups)

½ teaspoon salt

½ cup plain full-fat Greek yogurt

½ cup mayonnaise

1 cup sour cream

1 teaspoon dried dill

½ teaspoon garlic powder

¼ teaspoon cayenne pepper

1. Heat oil in a large skillet over medium-high heat. Add onion and salt. Stir-fry 20 minutes or until browned and starting to caramelize. Remove from heat to cool.
2. In a large bowl, whisk together remaining ingredients. Fold in onion.
3. Refrigerate until ready to serve.

Spinach Tots

These low-carb tots are a high-protein, vegetable-packed alternative to traditional tater tots, combining creamy cheese, savory spinach, and a touch of heat. Crispy outside and tender inside, they make a perfect snack or side dish without the carb crash.

Serves 6

Per Serving

Calories	151
Fat	11g
Sodium	294mg
Carbohydrates	5g
Fiber	2g
Sugar	1g
Protein	7g

1 (12-ounce) bag frozen chopped spinach, thawed
4 ounces cream cheese, softened
1 large egg, whisked
½ teaspoon prepared horseradish
¼ teaspoon salt
¼ teaspoon ground black pepper
⅓ cup almond flour
⅓ cup grated Parmesan cheese

1. Preheat oven to 400°F. Line a baking sheet with parchment paper.
2. Place spinach on a paper towel and squeeze out all excess water. Transfer to a medium bowl. Add cream cheese, egg, horseradish, salt, and black pepper. Form mixture into twelve balls.
3. On a small shallow plate, combine almond flour and Parmesan. Roll each ball in almond flour mixture. Shape into tots and place on baking sheet.
4. Bake 20 minutes. Spray tops of tots with nonstick butter spray. Place under broiler on high 2 minutes. Transfer to a serving dish and serve warm.

Buffalo Chicken Dip

Serves 6

Per Serving

Calories	531
Fat	42g
Sodium	497mg
Carbohydrates	4g
Fiber	0g
Sugar	3g
Protein	24g

This is a creamy, spicy appetizer made with shredded chicken, cream cheese, hot sauce, and ranch, baked until bubbly. It's perfect for game day or parties and is best served warm with carb-free chips or fresh-cut vegetables.

1 (8-ounce) block cream cheese, room temperature

8 ounces sour cream

1 cup Homemade Ranch Dressing (Chapter 9)

½ cup buffalo hot sauce

½ cup shredded sharp Cheddar cheese

2½ cups shredded cooked chicken breast

1. Preheat oven to 350°F.
2. In a medium bowl, combine cream cheese, sour cream, ranch dip, and hot sauce until smooth. Fold in shredded cheese and chicken.
3. Spoon mixture into a 13" × 9" ungreased baking dish and bake 10 minutes.
4. Let cool 10 minutes and serve warm.

Blue Cheese Dip

Yields 1½ cups

Per Serving (Serving size: ¼ cup)

Calories	95
Fat	7g
Sodium	133mg
Carbohydrates	2g
Fiber	0g
Sugar	2g
Protein	5g

Homemade blue cheese dip is not only easy to make but also guarantees you won't have the added sugars and preservatives that bottle varieties tend to contain.

1 cup plain full-fat Greek yogurt

2 tablespoons mayonnaise

⅓ cup blue cheese crumbles

1 teaspoon lemon juice

¼ teaspoon ground black pepper

½ teaspoon Worcestershire sauce

2 teaspoons dried chives

In a large bowl, combine all ingredients. Can be served immediately but is even better served chilled. Refrigerate, covered, up to 5 days.

Baked Pimento Cheese Jalapeño Poppers

Serves 8

Per Serving

Calories	227
Fat	20g
Sodium	403mg
Carbohydrates	2g
Fiber	0g
Sugar	1g
Protein	9g

These open-faced poppers are a bold, low-carb appetizer featuring spicy jalapeños stuffed with a creamy and tangy pimento cheese. Topped with crunchy crushed pork rinds and baked to golden perfection, they deliver the perfect balance of richness and heat.

1 cup crushed pork rinds

8 large jalapeño peppers, halved lengthwise and seeded

1½ cups Pimento Cheese (see recipe in this chapter)

1. Preheat oven to 350°F. Line a baking sheet with parchment paper.
2. Place crushed pork rinds on a small shallow plate.
3. Place halved jalapeños on baking sheet. Fill peppers with Pimento Cheese. Dip filled portions of peppers into pork rinds for a light coating and place on baking sheet.
4. Bake 30 minutes. Let rest 5 minutes. Serve warm.

Spinach and Crab Dip

Serves 8

Per Serving

Calories	245
Fat	19g
Sodium	454mg
Carbohydrates	4g
Fiber	0g
Sugar	2g
Protein	10g

This dip is a warm, creamy appetizer made with tender crabmeat, sautéed spinach, cream cheese, and savory seasonings. Baked until golden and bubbly, it's perfect for dipping with fresh-cut vegetables.

1 tablespoon unsalted butter

½ cup minced yellow onion

1 cup chopped baby spinach leaves

2 (8-ounce) packages cream cheese, room temperature

1 teaspoon Worcestershire sauce

½ teaspoon Old Bay Seasoning

½ pound lump crabmeat, cartilage removed

¼ cup shredded Parmesan cheese

1. Preheat oven to 350°F.
2. In a medium skillet, heat butter over medium-high heat. Add onion and cook 3 minutes or until onion is tender. Add spinach and toss an additional minute until spinach is wilted. Drain.
3. In a large bowl, add onions and spinach. Add cream cheese, Worcestershire sauce, Old Bay, and crabmeat and stir to combine. Place in an 8" × 8" ungreased baking dish. Bake 30 minutes.
4. Top with Parmesan cheese and place under a high-heat broiler 2 minutes or until cheese is browned. Serve warm.

Mini Cheese Balls

These mini cheese balls are a low-carb, snack loaded with creamy cheese, savory seasonings, and a crunchy coating of pecans and pork rinds. Perfect for parties or snacking, they deliver big flavor in a bite-sized package.

Yields 10 mini cheese balls

Per Serving (Serving size: 1 ball)

Calories	277
Fat	23g
Sodium	292mg
Carbohydrates	4g
Fiber	1g
Sugar	2g
Protein	10g

12 ounces cream cheese, room temperature
1 cup finely shredded Cheddar cheese
1⁄4 cup plain full-fat Greek yogurt
1 teaspoon garlic powder
1 teaspoon onion powder
1⁄4 teaspoon ground black pepper
1 cup finely chopped pecans
1⁄2 cup crushed pork rinds
2 tablespoons chopped fresh parsley

1. In a medium bowl, combine cream cheese, Cheddar cheese, yogurt, garlic powder, onion powder, and black pepper. Form into ten (2-tablespoon) balls.
2. On a medium shallow plate, combine pecans, pork rinds, and parsley. Roll balls in mixture to coat.
3. Refrigerate, covered, for 30 minutes. Serve chilled. Can be stored in refrigerator up to 2 days.

Roasted Red Pepper Hummus

Different from traditional hummus, this recipe includes roasted red peppers, which add notes of smokiness and a little sweetness. Enjoy this hummus with vegetables for dipping, and you can even offer slices of pita bread to guests who are not on your dietary path.

Yields 1½ cups

Per Serving (Serving size: ¼ cup)

Calories	188
Fat	12g
Sodium	196mg
Carbohydrates	15g
Fiber	4g
Sugar	3g
Protein	5g

1 (15-ounce) can chickpeas, drained and rinsed

¼ cup sesame tahini

¾ cup jarred roasted red peppers, divided

¼ cup lemon juice

3 tablespoons olive oil, divided

4 cloves garlic, peeled

½ teaspoon smoked paprika

½ teaspoon ground cumin

1. In a food processor, add chickpeas, tahini, ½ cup roasted red peppers, lemon juice, 2 tablespoons oil, garlic, paprika, and cumin. Pulse until smooth.
2. Transfer mixture to a serving bowl and drizzle with remaining oil. Dice remaining roasted red peppers and sprinkle on top of hummus. Serve.

Onion and Bacon Jam

Yields 3½ cups

Per Serving (Serving size: ¼ cup)

Calories	151
Fat	12g
Sodium	253mg
Carbohydrates	4g
Fiber	0g
Sugar	1g
Protein	5g

What Are True Caramelized Onions?

Most recipes will use the term "caramelized onions" when they actually mean "blond onions." Blond onions are cooked until they are tender and lightly browned. Caramelized onions are cooked for a longer time and achieve a rich brown color. Both add a delicious flavor, with the caramelized variety becoming almost jam-like.

This low-carb spread is bursting with smoky bacon, sweet caramelized onions, and bold spices. Perfect for topping burgers, eggs, or low-carb crackers, it delivers umami-filled indulgent flavor without the added sugar.

1 pound no-sugar-added bacon, quartered
2 medium yellow onions, peeled and sliced
4 cloves garlic, peeled and minced
¼ cup sugar-free barbecue sauce
¼ teaspoon maple extract
1 tablespoon Swerve brown sugar
2 teaspoons chili powder
1 teaspoon instant espresso powder
¼ cup shredded Parmesan cheese

1. In a large pot set over medium-high heat, add bacon, onions, and garlic and cook 25 minutes.
2. Add remaining ingredients and cook 20 minutes, stirring occasionally. Using an immersion blender, blend until smooth.
3. Bring pot ingredients to a boil. Reduce heat to low and simmer, uncovered, 30 minutes.
4. Serve warm or chilled. Can be refrigerated up to 2 weeks.

Pimento Cheese

This creamy, tangy Southern cheese spread is made with sharp Cheddar, diced pimientos, and a hint of spice. Used as a dip, sandwich filling, or vegetable topper, it's both comforting and versatile.

Yields 2½ cups

Per Serving (Serving size: ¼ cup)

Calories	251
Fat	23g
Sodium	401mg
Carbohydrates	2g
Fiber	0g
Sugar	1g
Protein	7g

1 (4-ounce) jar diced pimientos, including juice

1 cup mayonnaise

½ cup plain full-fat Greek yogurt

1 cup grated sharp Cheddar cheese

1 cup finely shredded Monterey jack cheese

½ teaspoon salt

1 teaspoon ground black pepper

1. In a medium bowl, combine all ingredients.
2. Serve chilled. Refrigerate, covered, up to 7 days.

Pimento Cheese Additions

If you'd like a little kick to this recipe, try adding a fresh, minced jalapeño pepper. If you don't want the kick but like texture and crunch, mince a little poblano or bell pepper into the cheese mix.

Honey Mustard Dipping Sauce

Yields 3/4 cup

Per Serving (Serving size: 1/4 cup)

Calories	155
Fat	14g
Sodium	272mg
Carbohydrates	7g
Fiber	0g
Sugar	6g
Protein	1g

Read Those Mayonnaise Labels!

All mayonnaise is not created equal. So many condiments on the shelves today are loaded with added sugars, so read those labels carefully. Brands that make a healthy product are readily available.

This dipping sauce blends sweet honey with tangy Dijon and yellow mustards for a smooth, zesty balance. The apple cider vinegar rounds out the flavor, making it a perfect sauce for baked chicken tenders, burgers, or vegetables.

1/4 cup mayonnaise

2 tablespoons yellow mustard

1 teaspoon Dijon mustard

1/4 teaspoon apple cider vinegar

1 tablespoon honey

1. In a small bowl, add all ingredients and mix until combined.
2. Serve immediately or store in a small lidded container and refrigerate up to 5 days.

Black Bean Hummus

This bold, creamy dip, made by blending black beans with tahini, lime juice, garlic, and spices, is a perfect Southwestern twist on traditional hummus. Packed with fiber and flavor, it's perfect for dipping vegetables, spreading on low-carb wraps, or serving with gluten-free chips.

Yields 1½ cups

Per Serving (Serving size: ¼ cup)

Calories	186
Fat	11g
Sodium	276mg
Carbohydrates	16g
Fiber	6g
Sugar	0g
Protein	6g

1 (15-ounce) can black beans, drained and rinsed

¼ cup sesame tahini

¼ cup lime juice

3 tablespoons olive oil, divided

4 cloves garlic, peeled

1 teaspoon chili powder

¼ teaspoon salt

2 tablespoons chopped fresh cilantro

1. In a food processor, add beans, tahini, lime juice, 2 tablespoons oil, garlic, chili powder, and salt. Pulse until smooth.
2. Transfer mixture to a serving bowl and drizzle with remaining oil. Garnish with cilantro. Serve.

Artichoke Heart Hummus

Yields 2 cups

Per Serving (Serving size: 1⁄4 cup)

Calories	147
Fat	9g
Sodium	284mg
Carbohydrates	13g
Fiber	4g
Sugar	2g
Protein	4g

Artichoke Heart Hummus is a creamy, tangy blend of chickpeas, marinated artichoke hearts, lemon juice, and garlic, offering a flavorful twist on classic hummus. Its bright and savory notes make it a perfect sandwich spread or Mediterranean-style dip for chopped vegetables.

1 (15-ounce) can chickpeas, drained and rinsed
1 (14-ounce) can artichoke hearts, drained
1⁄4 cup sesame tahini
1⁄4 cup lemon juice
3 tablespoons olive oil, divided
4 cloves garlic, peeled
1⁄4 teaspoon salt
1⁄4 teaspoon smoked paprika
2 tablespoons chopped fresh parsley

1. In a food processor, add chickpeas, artichoke hearts, tahini, lemon juice, 2 tablespoons oil, garlic, and salt. Pulse until smooth.
2. Transfer mixture to a serving bowl and drizzle with remaining oil. Sprinkle with paprika and garnish with parsley. Serve.

Raw Oysters with Cucumber Shallot Relish

Nestling your oyster shells in kosher salt will not only give you a dramatic and authentic presentation, but it will also help support the shells. Oysters are naturally low in carbs and high in protein and zinc, making them a nutrient-dense choice. Serve with sliced lemons for a splash of fresh citrus.

Serves 4

Per Serving

Calories	144
Fat	3g
Sodium	234mg
Carbohydrates	12g
Fiber	0g
Sugar	3g
Protein	15g

1 cup minced English cucumber

1 medium shallot, peeled and minced

½ cup apple cider vinegar

1 teaspoon honey

⅛ teaspoon salt

¼ teaspoon ground black pepper

1 teaspoon chopped fresh dill

1 dozen raw oysters, shucked

1. In a medium bowl, combine cucumber, shallot, vinegar, honey, salt, black pepper, and dill. Refrigerate relish 1 hour or up to overnight.
2. Spoon relish over shucked oysters. Serve chilled.

Finding Shucked Oysters

Most grocers sell pre-shucked oysters in containers, in which case you can purchase oyster shells online. Some specialty grocers have fresh oysters, and you can ask your fishmonger to shuck the oysters for you and save the shells for your presentation.

Chilled Shrimp Cocktail

Serves 4

Per Serving

Calories	114
Fat	1g
Sodium	1,450mg
Carbohydrates	8g
Fiber	2g
Sugar	6g
Protein	15g

What Is an Ice Bath?

An ice bath stops the cooking process almost immediately. Simply fill a metal bowl halfway with ice and add water to cover the ice. This is not only effective with chilled shrimp but also an excellent method to use for crisp vegetables.

Shrimp are an excellent source of protein and are so easy and quick to cook. For an individual appetizer presentation, use shallow stemmed glassware. Arrange shrimp around the perimeter of the glass with freshly made cocktail sauce in the middle.

2 bay leaves

1 tablespoon seafood seasoning

1 pound extra-large shrimp, peeled, deveined, tail on

1 cup Cocktail Sauce (Chapter 9)

1. Fill a large pot halfway with water. Stir in bay leaves and seafood seasoning and bring to a boil.
2. Add shrimp and cook 3 minutes or until shrimp are opaque. Remove and discard bay leaves. Drain shrimp and transfer to an ice bath. Let sit 5 minutes. Drain and pat dry.
3. Transfer shrimp to a platter or glassware and serve with Cocktail Sauce.

Steak Bites with Blue Cheese Crumbles

Serves 4

Per Serving

Calories	295
Fat	16g
Sodium	436mg
Carbohydrates	1g
Fiber	0g
Sugar	0g
Protein	34g

These tender and flavorful chunks of rib eye are seared to perfection after bathing in a tangy, savory marinade. Topped with creamy blue cheese crumbles, this dish delivers a bold, protein-packed bite perfect for an appetizer or even a main course.

1 tablespoon avocado oil

2 teaspoons Worcestershire sauce

1 tablespoon white vinegar

½ teaspoon salt

½ teaspoon garlic powder

½ teaspoon minced onion

2 (10-ounce) rib eye steaks, cut into 1-inch chunks

2 tablespoons blue cheese crumbles

1. In a medium bowl, combine oil, Worcestershire sauce, vinegar, salt, garlic powder, and onion. Add rib eye chunks and toss. Cover and refrigerate 30 minutes.
2. In a large skillet over medium-high heat, add rib eye chunks along with marinade. Stir-fry 3 minutes or until chunks are seared on all sides. Remove from heat and let rest 7 minutes.
3. Transfer chunks to a medium bowl and toss with blue cheese crumbles. Serve warm.

CHAPTER 4

Poultry

Whole Roasted Chicken 72
Chicken Thighs, Brussels Sprouts, and Pears 73
Chicken Lettuce Wraps 74
Chicken Gyro Bowls 75
Sheet Pan Drumsticks and Vegetables 77
Hasselback Chicken Breasts 78
Chicken Piccata 79
Bruschetta Chicken Tenders 80
Chicken Parmesan 81
Fajita-Style Chicken Kebabs 82
Island Chicken Thighs 84
Chicken Thighs with Creamy Dijon Sauce 85
Creamy Dill Chicken Bites 86
Easy Chicken Casserole 87
Chicken Meatballs with Pesto 89
Sloppy Turkey Janes 90
Enchilada Turkey Pie 91
Spicy Cabbage and Turkey Smoked Sausage 92
Quick Turkey Stir-Fry 94
Marinated Turkey Legs 95
Cornish Hens 96

Whole Roasted Chicken

Serves 4

Per Serving

Calories	294
Fat	19g
Sodium	655mg
Carbohydrates	1g
Fiber	0g
Sugar	0g
Protein	25g

What to Do with the Giblets?

If you have always thrown away that bag found in the chicken cavity, you are missing out! The giblets include the heart, liver, gizzard, and neck. Add the heart, gizzard, and neck to your bones when making chicken broth. Sauté the liver separately or make into a pâté, as it can turn bitter in a broth.

Roasting a whole chicken not only makes for a great family meal; it is also perfect for meal prepping at the beginning of the week. Packed with juicy flavor and naturally low in carbs and high in protein, this staple fits seamlessly into your high-protein, low-carb lifestyle. Use the leftover meat in salads or wraps or as snacks, and use the bones to make a broth or a soup recipe later in the week.

3 tablespoons unsalted butter, melted

1 teaspoon salt

½ teaspoon ground black pepper

½ teaspoon onion powder

½ teaspoon garlic powder

¼ teaspoon dried rosemary

1 (4-pound) whole chicken, giblets removed

½ medium yellow onion, peeled and cut into 3 wedges

½ medium orange, cut into 3 sections

1. Preheat oven to 425°F. Line a roasting pan with parchment paper.
2. In a medium bowl, whisk together butter, salt, black pepper, onion powder, garlic powder, and rosemary.
3. Add chicken to roasting pan and pat dry with paper towels. Brush butter mixture over entire chicken, including the cavity. Add onion wedges and orange sections to chicken cavity.
4. Bake 70 minutes or until internal temperature reaches 165°F. Let rest 10 minutes and serve.

Chicken Thighs, Brussels Sprouts, and Pears

Perfect for a cozy weeknight dinner, this dish is as flavorful as it is nutritious. High in protein and naturally low in carbs with smartly portioned fruit, this one-pan wonder is both balanced and satisfying.

Serves 4

Per Serving

Calories	487
Fat	26g
Sodium	784mg
Carbohydrates	23g
Fiber	6g
Sugar	11g
Protein	36g

4 bone-in, skin-on chicken thighs (1½ pounds total weight)

1 teaspoon salt

1 teaspoon ground black pepper

1 pound Brussels sprouts, quartered

2 tablespoons avocado oil

Juice from 1 medium navel orange

1 tablespoon orange zest

2 tablespoons grated Parmesan cheese

2 medium pears, seeded and thinly sliced

1. Preheat oven to 350°F. Line a rimmed baking sheet with parchment paper.
2. Add chicken thighs to half of baking sheet. Season with salt and black pepper.
3. In a medium bowl, toss Brussels sprouts with oil, orange juice, orange zest, and Parmesan cheese. Add to remaining half of baking sheet. Bake 45 minutes.
4. Toss Brussels sprouts again and add in pear slices. Bake an additional 15 minutes. Serve warm.

Chicken Lettuce Wraps

Serves 4

Per Serving

Calories	307
Fat	16g
Sodium	622mg
Carbohydrates	14g
Fiber	2g
Sugar	6g
Protein	25g

These healthy wraps feature seasoned ground chicken stir-fried with garlic, ginger, coconut aminos, and more and then spooned on crisp butter lettuce leaves for a fresh, low-carb bite. Topped with crushed peanuts, they make a light yet flavorful meal.

1 tablespoon sesame oil
1 pound ground chicken
1 small bunch green onions, sliced (white and green parts separated)
1 cup shredded carrots
1-inch piece fresh ginger, peeled and grated
1⁄4 cup coconut aminos
1 teaspoon fish sauce
1 tablespoon sriracha
1 teaspoon apple cider vinegar
2 teaspoons honey
4 cloves garlic, peeled and minced
1 medium head butter lettuce, leaves separated
4 tablespoons crushed peanuts

1. In a large skillet, heat oil over medium-high heat 1 minute. Add chicken, green onion whites, and carrots. Sauté 3–4 minutes until chicken is browned.
2. In a small bowl, whisk together ginger, coconut aminos, fish sauce, sriracha, vinegar, honey, and garlic. Pour mixture over chicken in skillet. Toss and heat through an additional minute.
3. Serve warm on lettuce leaves and garnish with green onion greens and crushed peanuts.

Chicken Gyro Bowls

This vibrant, Mediterranean low-carb dish is colorful, healthy, and satisfying. The tender chicken and array of vegetables are all typical ingredients in a classic gyro—the only thing missing is the pita!

Serves 4

Per Serving

Calories	448
Fat	27g
Sodium	1,492mg
Carbohydrates	14g
Fiber	3g
Sugar	8g
Protein	39g

¼ cup plain full-fat Greek yogurt
1 tablespoon Italian seasoning
Juice and zest from 1 medium lemon
1 teaspoon cumin
1 teaspoon garlic salt
1 pound boneless, skinless chicken breasts, cut into 1-inch cubes
1 tablespoon avocado oil
1 (8-ounce) bag shredded lettuce
1 cup diced cucumbers
2 medium Roma tomatoes, diced
1 cup diced red onion
1 cup chopped kalamata olives
1 cup feta cheese crumbles
1 cup Tzatziki Sauce (Chapter 9)

1. In a medium bowl, combine yogurt, Italian seasoning, lemon juice and zest, cumin, and garlic salt. Add chicken cubes and toss. Refrigerate, covered, 30 minutes or up to overnight.
2. In a large skillet, heat oil over medium-high heat. Add chicken and, flipping several times, cook 8 minutes or until internal temperature reaches 165°F. Remove from heat and let rest 5 minutes.
3. Distribute lettuce among individual serving bowls. Imagine each bowl is a pie and distribute chicken and remaining ingredients except for Tzatziki Sauce in their own pie section, then add a big dollop of the sauce in the middle. Serve.

Kalamata Olives versus Black Olives

Although black olives are a perfectly acceptable substitute for kalamatas, they are saltier and milder in flavor. Kalamata olives are deeper in color and known for their tangy and slightly fruity flavor. Because they are often cured in a red wine or vinegar brine, they have a more complex taste.

Sheet Pan Drumsticks and Vegetables

This one-and-done sheet pan meal is a real time-saver on those busy weeknights. Here you'll get the healthy carbs from the vegetables combined with the filling protein from the drumsticks. The dark meat of drumsticks makes for a tender and flavor-filled dish. The outer crunchiness and inner tenderness of the vegetables round out the texture of this dish perfectly.

Serves 4

Per Serving

Calories	701
Fat	41g
Sodium	923mg
Carbohydrates	10g
Fiber	3g
Sugar	4g
Protein	63g

1⁄3 cup avocado oil

1 teaspoon salt

1⁄2 teaspoon ground black pepper

1⁄2 teaspoon garlic powder

1⁄4 teaspoon cayenne pepper

3 pounds bone-in, skin-on chicken drumsticks

2 medium red onions, peeled and cut into 6 wedges

3 cups roughly chopped broccoli (florets and stems)

1. Preheat oven to 425°F. Line a rimmed baking sheet with parchment paper.
2. In a large bowl, whisk together oil, salt, black pepper, garlic powder, and cayenne pepper.
3. Add chicken, red onions, and broccoli to oil mixture and toss to coat. Place on baking sheet.
4. Bake 35 minutes or until chicken is cooked through, and then broil on high 2 minutes to crisp chicken skin.
5. Transfer to plates and serve warm.

Pre-Cut Broccoli

If chopping vegetables is not in your plan book, you can purchase bagged, pre-cut broccoli in the produce aisle of most grocery stores.

Hasselback Chicken Breasts

Serves 3

Per Serving

Calories	716
Fat	28g
Sodium	996mg
Carbohydrates	10g
Fiber	0g
Sugar	4g
Protein	102g

A beautifully impressive dish that's easy to prepare, these juicy chicken breasts are sliced and stuffed with roasted red peppers and fresh mozzarella. Pre-prepared or jarred pesto lends all the Italian-inspired flavor. This dish has minimal carbs and yet maximum satisfaction.

3 chicken breasts (approximately 2½ pounds total)

¼ cup pesto

8 ounces fresh mozzarella, sliced into 12 half-moons

6 ounces jarred roasted red peppers

1. Preheat oven to 350°F. Spray a 9" × 13" baking dish with nonstick cooking spray.
2. Score each chicken breast with four slits per breast and place in baking dish.
3. Brush pesto over chicken. Tuck 1 slice mozzarella and roasted red peppers into each slit.
4. Bake chicken breasts 25 minutes. Let rest 5 minutes. Serve warm.

Chicken Piccata

This classic dish is easy to make and delicious. And those little salty bombs called capers add amazing flavor and make this dish feel fancy with minimal effort. Because it is typically made with a lean protein like chicken or fish, this dish is also high in protein. Serve with a side of mashed cauliflower or steamed broccoli for a complete, low-carb meal.

Serves 4

Per Serving

Calories	285
Fat	17g
Sodium	666mg
Carbohydrates	4g
Fiber	3g
Sugar	1g
Protein	29g

4 (4-ounce) boneless, skinless chicken breasts, sliced in half lengthwise

1/4 cup almond flour

1/4 cup flaxseed meal

1/2 teaspoon salt

1/2 teaspoon ground black pepper

3 tablespoons unsalted butter, divided

1 cup chicken broth

Juice from 1/2 large lemon

1/2 large lemon, thinly sliced into rounds

2 tablespoons capers, drained

2 tablespoons chopped parsley

1. Place each chicken breast half between two pieces of parchment paper and pound to even out the chicken.
2. In a small bowl, combine flour, flaxseed meal, salt, and black pepper. Dredge each piece of chicken in mixture. Set aside.
3. In a large skillet, heat 1 tablespoon butter over medium-high heat. Add 4 pieces of chicken and cook 3 minutes per side. Repeat with 1 tablespoon butter and remaining chicken. Place cooked chicken on a large serving dish.
4. In the same skillet, add broth, lemon juice, lemon rounds, capers, and remaining butter. Cook over medium heat 3 minutes, scraping the brown bits off the bottom of the skillet. Remove skillet from heat and let rest 3 minutes.
5. Spoon mixture over cooked chicken. Garnish with parsley and serve warm.

Bruschetta Chicken Tenders

Serves 4

Per Serving

Calories	270
Fat	17g
Sodium	556mg
Carbohydrates	3g
Fiber	1g
Sugar	2g
Protein	24g

What Are Chicken Tenders?

Also called chicken tenderloins, chicken tenders are small, thin strips of chicken meat loosely attached to the underside of the chicken breast. Although tenders are more delicate, if you cannot find them at a grocery store, you can buy chicken breasts and thinly slice them on your own.

Traditionally served on carb-filled crusty bread, this new take on an Italian classic serves the zesty tomato bruschetta on chicken tenders instead. This easy and delicious dish brings all the flavor of the original but with less carbs.

Bruschetta

4 medium Roma tomatoes, diced

1⁄4 cup olive oil

1⁄4 cup chopped fresh basil

1 tablespoon white wine vinegar

2 cloves garlic, peeled and minced

1⁄4 teaspoon salt

Chicken Tenders

1 tablespoon avocado oil

1 1⁄2 pounds chicken breast tenders

1⁄2 teaspoon salt

1⁄2 teaspoon ground black pepper

1. For the bruschetta: In a medium bowl, combine all ingredients. Refrigerate until ready to use.
2. For the chicken tenders: In a large skillet, heat oil over medium-high heat. Add chicken, season with salt and black pepper, and cook 6 minutes, flipping after 3 minutes or until internal temperature reaches 165°F. Remove from heat and let rest 5 minutes.
3. Transfer chicken tenders to a serving dish and top with bruschetta. Serve.

Chicken Parmesan

This simple high-protein dish is great as is or served over spaghetti squash noodles (see recipe in sidebar).

Serves 6

Per Serving

Calories	312
Fat	18g
Sodium	573mg
Carbohydrates	8g
Fiber	1g
Sugar	5g
Protein	28g

3 (6-ounce) boneless, skinless chicken breasts, sliced in half lengthwise

½ cup plain full-fat Greek yogurt

¼ cup almond flour

¼ cup grated Parmesan cheese

2 tablespoons avocado oil

1 (24-ounce) jar marinara sauce

1 cup grated mozzarella

¼ cup chopped fresh basil

1. Preheat oven to 350°F. Place each chicken breast half between two pieces of parchment paper and pound to an even thickness.
2. Brush both sides of chicken with yogurt.
3. In a medium bowl, combine flour and Parmesan cheese. Dip chicken in Parmesan mixture.
4. In a large skillet, heat oil over medium-high heat and brown chicken on each side 2 minutes. Add 18 ounces (¾ jar) marinara sauce to a 9" × 13" ungreased baking dish. Add browned chicken to dish. Pour remaining sauce over chicken. Top with mozzarella cheese. Cook 10 minutes.
5. Let rest 10 minutes. Garnish with basil and serve warm.

Easy Spaghetti Squash Noodles

Slice a medium spaghetti squash horizontally. Brush with 1 tablespoon avocado oil and bake 50 minutes in a 375°F oven. Let cool enough to handle. Using a fork, scrape inside of squash to reveal the "spaghetti" strands.

Fajita-Style Chicken Kebabs

Serves 4

Per Serving

Calories	343
Fat	24g
Sodium	711mg
Carbohydrates	8g
Fiber	2g
Sugar	3g
Protein	21g

Metal versus Wooden Skewers

Either type of skewer is acceptable; however, you should soak your wooden or bamboo skewers in warm water for 30 minutes prior to piercing your foods.

Bursting with bold Tex-Mex flavors, these kebabs are loaded with marinated chicken and colorful red onion and poblano pepper, all grilled to smoky perfection on skewers. The juice and zest from the clementines balance out the spicy flavors.

¼ cup avocado oil
1 tablespoon hot sauce
Juice of 1 large lime
1 teaspoon grated lime zest
Juice of 1 small clementine
1 teaspoon grated clementine zest
½ cup chopped cilantro
1 teaspoon salt
1 teaspoon cumin
¼ teaspoon chili powder
1 pound boneless, skinless chicken thighs, cut into 1-inch cubes
1 medium red onion, peeled and cut into 1-inch chunks
1 poblano pepper, seeded and cut into 1-inch chunks
1 (8-ounce) pack whole white mushrooms

1. In a large bowl, whisk together oil, hot sauce, lime juice, lime zest, clementine juice, clementine zest, cilantro, salt, cumin, and chili powder. Add chicken cubes and toss. Refrigerate 30 minutes.
2. Add onion, poblano pepper, and mushrooms to bowl and toss. Refrigerate an additional 30 minutes.
3. Skewer meat and vegetables on skewers, alternating ingredients.
4. Heat a grill or grilling pan over medium-high heat. Place skewers on grill and cook 2–3 minutes per side until chicken is cooked through, about 10 minutes total. Remove from grill and let rest 5 minutes. Serve warm.

Island Chicken Thighs

Serves 6

Per Serving

Calories	440
Fat	28g
Sodium	251mg
Carbohydrates	8g
Fiber	0g
Sugar	6g
Protein	33g

Canned Coconut Milk versus Carton Coconutmilk

In short, canned coconut milk should be used in cooking, while carton Coconutmilk is more for drinking. The canned variety is thick and rich, made from grated coconut meat and water. Carton Coconutmilk is thinner and often contains added sugars.

These juicy chicken thighs soak up all the vibrancy of tropical island flavors. You may even want to move these to the backyard grill on a summer night for a tropical staycation. Serve with grilled asparagus or a spring mix salad and your favorite homemade dressing.

1 cup canned coconut milk

1 (8-ounce) can crushed pineapple, including juice

1 tablespoon avocado oil

1 tablespoon sriracha

1 tablespoon coconut aminos

1 (1-inch) piece fresh ginger, minced

1½ pounds chicken thighs (about 6 thighs)

1. In a food processor, pulse together coconut milk, pineapple and juice, oil, sriracha, coconut aminos, and ginger. Add to a large bowl, then add chicken thighs. Toss. Cover and refrigerate 30 minutes.
2. Preheat oven to 400°F. Line a 9" × 13" baking dish with parchment paper.
3. Add thighs to baking dish and bake 25 minutes or until internal temperature reaches 165°F.
4. Let rest 7 minutes and serve warm.

Chicken Thighs with Creamy Dijon Sauce

This high-protein dish is elegant enough for guests but simple enough for weeknight cooking.

Serves 6

Per Serving

Calories	411
Fat	27g
Sodium	590mg
Carbohydrates	1g
Fiber	0g
Sugar	0g
Protein	33g

1⁄4 cup heavy cream

1⁄4 cup Dijon mustard

2 tablespoons plain full-fat Greek yogurt

1⁄2 teaspoon salt

1⁄4 teaspoon ground black pepper

2 tablespoons unsalted butter

1 1⁄2 pounds chicken thighs (about 6 thighs)

1⁄4 cup chopped fresh parsley

1. In a medium bowl, whisk together cream, mustard, yogurt, salt, and black pepper. Set aside.
2. In a large skillet over medium-high heat, add butter. Add chicken and cook 5 minutes. Flip chicken and cook an additional 5 minutes.
3. Add cream mixture. Bring to a boil. Reduce heat to low and simmer 10 minutes or until internal temperature of chicken reaches 165°F.
4. Let rest 7 minutes. Garnish with parsley and serve warm.

Creamy Dill Chicken Bites

Serves 2

Per Serving

Calories	561
Fat	33g
Sodium	926mg
Carbohydrates	9g
Fiber	1g
Sugar	3g
Protein	54g

These tender chicken cubes, pan-seared and simmered in a smooth, creamy sauce, are a quick and flavorful weeknight dish. The fresh dill adds a bright, herbaceous finish that perfectly complements the cream base. These are delicious served with roasted asparagus.

½ teaspoon salt

½ teaspoon ground black pepper

¼ cup chickpea flour

1 pound chicken breasts, cut into 1-inch cubes

1 tablespoon avocado oil

½ cup heavy cream

½ cup chicken broth

¼ cup chopped fresh dill, divided

1. In a medium bowl, combine salt, black pepper, and flour. Add chicken cubes and toss to coat. Remove chicken and shake off any excess flour mixture.
2. In a large skillet, heat oil. Add chicken and stir-fry 5 minutes or until brown on all sides. Transfer to a plate.
3. To the same skillet, add cream, broth, and 2 tablespoons dill. Bring to a rolling boil, scraping brown bits off the bottom of the pan. Reduce heat to low and simmer 5 minutes to reduce and thicken the sauce. Add chicken. Continue to simmer 5 minutes.
4. Let rest 5 minutes. Transfer to individual serving bowls, garnish with remaining dill, and serve warm.

Easy Chicken Casserole

This casserole is pure comfort food. The rich blend of yogurt, mayonnaise, and cream keeps it low in carbs while delivering a punch of protein with the chicken and bacon. Tossed with spinach and onion for a vegetable boost, this dish is a busy weeknight winner!

Serves 4

Per Serving

Calories	642
Fat	41g
Sodium	1,289mg
Carbohydrates	5g
Fiber	1g
Sugar	2g
Protein	53g

½ cup plain full-fat Greek yogurt

¼ cup mayonnaise

2 tablespoons heavy cream

1 teaspoon salt

½ teaspoon ground black pepper

½ teaspoon garlic powder

1 teaspoon dried dill

1 teaspoon Italian seasoning

3 cups diced cooked chicken

3 slices no-sugar-added bacon, cooked and crumbled

2 cups shredded Cheddar cheese, divided

1 tablespoon avocado oil

1 small yellow onion, peeled and diced

3 cups baby spinach leaves

1. Preheat oven to 350°F. Spray a 9" × 13" baking dish with nonstick cooking spray.
2. In a medium bowl, combine yogurt, mayonnaise, cream, salt, black pepper, garlic powder, dill, Italian seasoning, chicken, bacon, and 1 cup Cheddar cheese.
3. In a large skillet, heat oil over medium-high heat. Add onion and cook 2 minutes or until tender. Add spinach leaves and cook 2–3 minutes until wilted. Cool, drain, and add to yogurt mixture. Stir to combine.
4. Add to baking dish and top with remaining cheese. Bake 25 minutes. Let rest 10 minutes and serve warm.

Chicken Meatballs with Pesto

Although store-bought versions of pesto are available at your grocery store, this cookbook has three different pesto recipes you could choose from for this recipe (see Chapter 9). Choose one to your liking or try a new one each week! With homemade pesto, the type of nuts and/or herbs can be interchanged in equal amounts depending on the season or your taste buds.

Serves 4

Per Serving

Calories	303
Fat	20g
Sodium	255mg
Carbohydrates	5g
Fiber	1g
Sugar	2g
Protein	24g

1 pound ground chicken

1 small yellow onion, peeled and grated

1 medium carrot, scrubbed and grated

3 tablespoons pesto, divided

3 tablespoons grated Parmesan cheese, divided

2 tablespoons avocado oil

1 tablespoon water

1. In a large bowl, combine chicken, onion, carrot, 1 tablespoon pesto, and 1 tablespoon Parmesan. Form into eight equal meatballs.
2. In a cast iron pan, heat avocado oil over medium-high heat. Add meatballs and cook about 5 minutes, turning to brown on all sides. Add water and reduce to a simmer. Cover and simmer an additional 4 minutes or until the internal temperature reaches 165°F.
3. Transfer meatballs to a large bowl. Toss with remaining pesto. Garnish with remaining Parmesan. Serve warm.

Sloppy Turkey Janes

Serves 4

Per Serving

Calories	332
Fat	15g
Sodium	980mg
Carbohydrates	25g
Fiber	3g
Sugar	15g
Protein	29g

Made with lean ground turkey simmered in a tangy tomato-based sauce, this one-pot wonder is a healthy twist on the classic sloppy joe. Count on making this easy recipe each week, served either as is or on a low-carb bun or alongside some fresh fruit.

1 tablespoon avocado oil

1 pound ground turkey

1 small yellow onion, peeled and grated

8 ounces white mushrooms, sliced

1 medium carrot, scrubbed and grated

½ teaspoon salt

½ teaspoon ground black pepper

1 tablespoon Swerve brown sugar

1 (15-ounce) can tomato sauce

2 tablespoons tomato paste

1 tablespoon Worcestershire sauce

1 tablespoon sriracha

1. In a large skillet, heat oil over medium-high heat. Add turkey and cook 5 minutes or until browned.
2. Reduce heat to medium and add onion, mushrooms, and carrot. Cook an additional 3 minutes or until onions are tender. Add remaining ingredients.
3. Bring to a boil. Reduce heat to low and simmer, uncovered, 20 minutes. Serve warm.

Enchilada Turkey Pie

Enjoy this comforting, layered casserole made with seasoned ground turkey, enchilada sauce, and cheese, all baked between low-carb tortillas. It's a hearty dish that delivers all the flavor of enchiladas with the ease of a one-pan meal.

Serves 6

Per Serving

Calories	498
Fat	27g
Sodium	1,289mg
Carbohydrates	33g
Fiber	14g
Sugar	7g
Protein	35g

2 tablespoons avocado oil
1 pound ground turkey
1 tablespoon ground cumin
1 tablespoon chili powder
1 small red onion, peeled and diced
4 (8-inch) low-carb tortillas
1 (10-ounce) can red enchilada sauce
1 (15-ounce) can refried black beans
2 cups shredded Mexican cheese blend
2 large beefsteak tomatoes, diced
½ teaspoon salt
¼ teaspoon ground black pepper
1 (8-ounce) bag shredded lettuce
½ cup sour cream

1. Preheat oven to 350°F.
2. In a large skillet, heat oil over medium-high heat and add turkey, cumin, chili powder, and onion. Cook 4 minutes, pushing turkey around skillet to brown.
3. Spray a 10-inch cake pan with nonstick cooking spray. Add a tortilla to the pan. Add half a can of enchilada sauce. Add a third of the cooked turkey mixture, then another tortilla. Spread with a third of refried beans. Add ⅓ cup cheese. Repeat layers, starting with the cooked turkey mixture. Top with remaining cooked turkey mixture, remaining tortilla, and remaining refried beans and pour in remaining enchilada sauce. Scatter remaining cheese over top.
4. Bake 30 minutes. Remove from oven and let rest 15 minutes.
5. Season tomatoes with salt and black pepper and toss to coat.
6. Slice pie and serve warm with tomatoes, shredded lettuce, and sour cream on the side.

Spicy Cabbage and Turkey Smoked Sausage

Serves 4

Per Serving

Calories	266
Fat	17g
Sodium	940mg
Carbohydrates	11g
Fiber	4g
Sugar	6g
Protein	14g

Gochujang versus Sriracha

Although both condiments are derived from red chili peppers, gochujang gets that fun and funky flavor from fermented soybean paste, whereas sriracha gets its umami from garlic. Both are delicious, and either can be used in this recipe.

This entire meal comes together in 10 minutes! Packed with flavor and protein, this bowl of goodness is as easy as it gets.

2 tablespoons avocado oil

1 (13-ounce) turkey smoked sausage, cut into ½-inch slices

4 cups shredded cabbage and carrot coleslaw mix

1 tablespoon gochujang

½ teaspoon salt

1. In a large skillet, heat oil over medium-high heat and add sausage slices. Cook 5 minutes, pushing sausage around skillet to brown sides.
2. Add coleslaw mix, gochujang, and salt and sauté 5 minutes or until cabbage begins to soften.
3. Add to individual serving bowls and serve warm.

Quick Turkey Stir-Fry

Serves 4

Per Serving

Calories	336
Fat	16g
Sodium	625mg
Carbohydrates	18g
Fiber	3g
Sugar	12g
Protein	27g

A flavorful meal perfect for busy nights, this stir-fry contains lean ground turkey and a colorful mix of vegetables. The savory-sweet sauce made with coconut aminos, sriracha, and a touch of honey adds bold flavor without piling on the carbs. High in protein and ready in minutes, it's a healthy and satisfying one-pan dinner.

2 tablespoons sesame oil, divided

1 pound ground turkey

1 (16-ounce) bag frozen stir-fry vegetables

2 tablespoons coconut aminos

2 teaspoons sriracha

2 teaspoons honey

½ teaspoon ground ginger

½ teaspoon garlic powder

½ teaspoon salt

2 tablespoons water

1. Add 1 tablespoon oil to a large skillet over medium heat. Add turkey and cook 5 minutes or until browned and crumbly. Transfer turkey to a plate.
2. In the same skillet, add remaining tablespoon oil and vegetables. Stir-fry 6 minutes or until vegetables start to soften. Return turkey to skillet. Add remaining ingredients. Stir-fry an additional 5 minutes.
3. Transfer to plates and serve warm.

Marinated Turkey Legs

Why wait until the holidays to enjoy turkey when you can enjoy it all year long? Lean turkey is a great option for those looking to build muscle, manage weight, or follow a low-carb diet.

Serves 2

Per Serving

Calories	1,164
Fat	50g
Sodium	536mg
Carbohydrates	2g
Fiber	0g
Sugar	1g
Protein	152g

1 (10.5-ounce) can mandarin oranges in juice

1⁄4 cup avocado oil

1 teaspoon salt

1 teaspoon onion powder

1⁄2 teaspoon cayenne pepper

2 cloves garlic, peeled

1⁄4 cup fresh parsley leaves

2 medium turkey legs

1. In a food processor or blender, pulse mandarin oranges and juice, oil, salt, onion powder, cayenne pepper, garlic, and parsley until smooth. Add marinade to a large plastic bag along with turkey legs. Let turkey legs marinate overnight, flipping bag over once.
2. Preheat oven to 375°F. Line a rimmed baking sheet with parchment paper.
3. Add marinated turkey legs to baking sheet. Bake 55 minutes or until internal temperature reaches 165°F.
4. Let rest 10 minutes. Serve warm.

Cornish Hens

Serves 2

Per Serving

Calories	796
Fat	56g
Sodium	2,489mg
Carbohydrates	2g
Fiber	0g
Sugar	0g
Protein	58g

These tender, miniature chickens are roasted whole for an elegant yet simple meal. Their small size makes them perfect for individual servings and impressive dinner presentations. Don't forget to save the carcass to make some chicken broth!

2 tablespoons avocado oil

2 Cornish hens, thawed

2 teaspoons salt

1 teaspoon ground black pepper

1 teaspoon garlic powder

2 clementines, halved

1. Preheat oven to 400°F. Line a baking sheet with parchment paper.
2. Massage oil over both Cornish hens. Season with salt, black pepper, and garlic powder. Stuff two clementine halves into each hen cavity. Place on baking sheet.
3. Bake 1 hour. Remove clementine halves and let hens rest 7 minutes. Serve warm.

CHAPTER 5

Beef, Pork, and Lamb

Bunless Beef Sliders 98
Mini Meatloaves 99
Margarita Flank Steak 100
Taco Meatzza 101
Beef and Broccoli 103
Cowboy Sirloin Steaks 104
Sweet Pepper Steak 105
No-Noodle Beef Stroganoff 106
Beef Soft Tacos 107
Philly Cheesesteak Bowls 108
Sloppy Joe Casserole 110
Mozzarella-Stuffed Meatballs 111
Stuffed Beefsteak Tomatoes 112
Oven Pulled Pork 113
Thai Burger Patties with Quick-Pickled Vegetables 115
Pork Egg Roll Bowl 116
Roasted Pork Tenderloin 117
Skillet Pork Chops with Plums 118
Mushroom and Swiss-Stuffed Pork Chops 119
Baked Baby Back Pork Ribs 120
Garlic Basil Frenched Rack of Lamb 122
Lamb Burgers 123

Bunless Beef Sliders

Serves 8

Per Serving

Calories	126
Fat	7g
Sodium	326mg
Carbohydrates	1g
Fiber	0g
Sugar	0g
Protein	11g

Who needs a high-carb bun when the meat is the star? The grated onion lends a moistness to the beef in these sliders, and no one will know you snuck it in. You can always add a lettuce wrap around each slider if you want to pick it up!

1 pound 80/20 ground beef

⅓ cup peeled and grated yellow onion

1 teaspoon smoked paprika

1 teaspoon salt

½ teaspoon garlic powder

½ teaspoon ground black pepper

1 tablespoon avocado oil

1. In a medium bowl, combine all ingredients except oil. Form into eight patties. Make a slight indentation in the middle of each.
2. Add avocado oil to a large skillet and set over medium-high heat.
3. Place patties in skillet and cook 2–3 minutes per side, depending on your preferred doneness.
4. Transfer to a large plate and let rest 5 minutes before serving warm.

Mini Meatloaves

Making mini meatloaves instead of one big one not only allows for quicker cooking and the probability the meat won't dry out during the cooking process, but also allows each person to get those delicious crispy edges where flavor is formed. This recipe uses low-carb bread to help reduce the carbs of traditional meatloaf.

Serves 6

Per Serving

Calories	360
Fat	20g
Sodium	1,280mg
Carbohydrates	10g
Fiber	5g
Sugar	3g
Protein	34g

¼ cup whole milk

1 tablespoon coconut aminos

2 large eggs

3 slices low-carb white bread, cubed

1 pound ground chuck

1 pound ground pork

1 cup no-sugar-added ketchup, divided

4 tablespoons yellow mustard, divided

1 teaspoon salt

1 teaspoon ground black pepper

1 teaspoon garlic powder

1 teaspoon cayenne pepper

1 tablespoon dried Italian seasoning

1. Preheat oven to 375°F. Line a rimmed baking sheet with parchment paper.
2. In a large bowl, whisk together milk, coconut aminos, and eggs. Toss in cubed bread to soften.
3. Add ground beef, ground pork, ½ cup ketchup, 2 tablespoons mustard, salt, black pepper, garlic powder, cayenne pepper, and Italian seasoning. Combine thoroughly without overworking. Form into six equal loaves and place on an ungreased baking sheet with edges.
4. In a small bowl, combine remaining ketchup and remaining mustard. Brush over the top of each meatloaf.
5. Bake 30 minutes or until internal temperature reaches 160°F. Serve warm.

Margarita Flank Steak

Serves 6

Per Serving

Calories	397
Fat	26g
Sodium	127mg
Carbohydrates	0g
Fiber	0g
Sugar	0g
Protein	34g

Although flank steak is one of the most inexpensive cuts of beef, it can be one of the most flavorful if done right. Originating from the cow's belly muscles, this cut of meat can be tough, but paired with the right marinade and thinly sliced against the grain, it may very well become your new favorite!

½ cup white tequila
¼ cup coconut aminos
¼ cup avocado oil
Juice and zest from 2 medium limes
Juice and zest from 1 medium navel orange
1 tablespoon Tabasco hot sauce
4 cloves garlic, peeled and minced
1 small bunch cilantro, rinsed and chopped
1 teaspoon salt
2 pounds flank steak

1. In a gallon plastic bag, combine all ingredients. Massage flavorings into flank steak and refrigerate 2 hours or up to overnight.
2. Heat a grilling pan over medium-high heat and add flank steak. Grill approximately 6 minutes per side, depending on your preferred doneness.
3. Remove flank steak from pan and let rest 7 minutes on a cutting board. Thinly slice against the grain and serve warm.

Taco Meatzza

We all love pizza, and now with this dish you can have all the flavors without any of the high-carb crust. Using this same beef crust, let your imagination go wild with the toppings, week after week. Consider making mini beef crusts and letting your family and friends curate their own pizzas!

Serves 6	
Per Serving	
Calories	348
Fat	20g
Sodium	1,256mg
Carbohydrates	10g
Fiber	2g
Sugar	7g
Protein	24g

1 pound 80/20 ground beef

2 teaspoons cumin

1 teaspoon salt

1 teaspoon smoked paprika

2 cups grated Mexican-style cheese, divided

2 cups canned enchilada sauce, divided

2 medium Roma tomatoes, diced

2 cups shredded lettuce

½ cup sour cream

1. Preheat oven to 400°F. Line a rimmed baking sheet with parchment paper.
2. In a large bowl, combine beef, cumin, salt, paprika, 1 cup cheese, and ½ cup enchilada sauce. On baking sheet, press meat into a circle about ⅛ inch thick.
3. Bake 15 minutes. Remove from oven and dab oil from off meat "crust." Let rest 10 minutes.
4. Spread remaining enchilada sauce on crust. Top with remaining cheese, tomatoes, lettuce, and dollops of sour cream.
5. Slice and serve warm.

Beef and Broccoli

This Asian American classic is traditionally thickened with cornstarch or flour, but xanthan gum, easily found in the baking aisle at most grocers, is a perfect gluten- and grain-free alternative.

Serves 4

Per Serving

Calories	352
Fat	20g
Sodium	329mg
Carbohydrates	11g
Fiber	3g
Sugar	3g
Protein	28g

1 tablespoon hot water

½ teaspoon xanthan gum

¼ cup coconut aminos

½ cup beef broth, divided

½ teaspoon ground ginger

1 teaspoon honey

4 cloves garlic, peeled and minced

3 tablespoons sesame oil, divided

1 pound sirloin, thinly sliced and cut into 1-inch lengths

3 cups chopped broccoli

1 small white onion, peeled and thinly sliced

2 teaspoons toasted sesame seeds

1. In a large bowl, make a slurry by whisking together water and xanthan gum. Whisk in coconut aminos, ¼ cup broth, ginger, honey, garlic, and 2 tablespoons sesame oil. Add sirloin, cover, and set aside in the refrigerator to marinate 30 minutes.
2. In a large skillet, heat remaining sesame oil over medium-high heat. Add broccoli and onion and stir-fry 3 minutes. Add remaining broth and simmer, covered, 3 minutes. Transfer broccoli and onion to a plate.
3. In same skillet over medium-high heat, add sirloin along with marinade. Stir-fry 3 minutes or until beef is cooked through. Add broccoli and onion mixture and stir-fry an additional minute. Let rest 2 minutes to allow sauce to thicken.
4. Serve warm garnished with sesame seeds.

Cowboy Sirloin Steaks

Serves 4

Per Serving

Calories	597
Fat	31g
Sodium	475mg
Carbohydrates	3g
Fiber	1g
Sugar	0g
Protein	62g

A Meat Thermometer Is Your Friend

Taking the guesswork out of cooking, a meat thermometer is essential for ensuring food safety by accurately measuring the internal temperature of meat, preventing undercooking. It also helps avoid overcooking, preserving the meat's juiciness and flavor. Resting meats after cooking is important, and because meat continues to cook during the resting phase, knowing what temperature to stop actively cooking it at is crucial.

These steaks are boldly seasoned with a smoky, spicy rub featuring chili powder, espresso powder, and warm spices for a deep, complex flavor. Pan-seared to juicy perfection, this meal delivers a hearty, high-protein punch with a rugged flair.

4 (10-ounce) sirloin steaks, 1 inch thick
1 tablespoon chili powder
2 teaspoons instant espresso powder
2 teaspoons smoked paprika
1 teaspoon garlic powder
1 teaspoon dry mustard
½ teaspoon salt
⅛ teaspoon cayenne pepper
⅛ teaspoon ground cinnamon
1 tablespoon avocado oil

1. Pat steaks dry with paper towels and allow to rest on the counter while you prep the rub.
2. In a small bowl, combine chili powder, espresso powder, paprika, garlic powder, mustard, salt, cayenne pepper, and cinnamon. Rub over steaks and let rest at room temperature 30 minutes.
3. Heat oil in a cast iron skillet over medium-high heat. Add sirloin steaks and cook 2 minutes per side. Using tongs, grasp steaks and roll them along their edges another 2 minutes approximately. If medium-rare is your goal, the internal temperature should be 130°F.
4. Transfer steaks to a cutting board and let rest 10 minutes. Serve warm.

Sweet Pepper Steak

This savory-sweet stir-fry features tender strips of flank steak and vibrant baby sweet peppers and onions. Simmered in a sauce kissed with ginger and balsamic vinegar, it's both colorful and packed with bold flavor.

Serves 6

Per Serving

Calories	237
Fat	10g
Sodium	506mg
Carbohydrates	6g
Fiber	1g
Sugar	2g
Protein	27g

2 tablespoons avocado oil

1 tablespoon balsamic vinegar

1 teaspoon salt

1 teaspoon ground black pepper

1 (1½-pound) flank steak, sliced against the grain into ¼-inch-thick strips

2½ cups thinly sliced baby sweet peppers

1 large yellow onion, peeled and thinly sliced

1 cup beef broth

1 tablespoon chickpea flour

2 tablespoons coconut aminos

1 teaspoon grated fresh ginger

1. In a large bowl, mix together oil, vinegar, salt, and black pepper. Toss steak strips in mixture and set aside 30 minutes.
2. In a large skillet over medium-high heat, add steak strips. Stir-fry 3 minutes or until browned but not cooked through. Transfer to a plate.
3. Add sweet peppers and onion to same skillet and stir-fry over medium-high heat 2 minutes or until onion is tender.
4. In a small bowl, whisk together broth and flour. Add coconut aminos and ginger. Pour mixture over peppers and onion. Return steak strips to skillet and stir to combine.
5. Cook an additional 3 minutes. Serve warm.

Baby Sweet Pepper Substitutions

If your produce section doesn't offer one of those pre-packaged bags of baby sweet peppers, mature bell peppers are an option. Each color has a slightly different flavor profile, so purchase one of each for a variety of flavors.

No-Noodle Beef Stroganoff

Serves 4

Per Serving

Calories	362
Fat	19g
Sodium	603mg
Carbohydrates	9g
Fiber	1g
Sugar	5g
Protein	32g

Slicing Beef Against the Grain

Slicing meat against the grain means cutting perpendicular to the direction of the muscle fibers, which shortens them and makes the meat more tender and easier to chew. This technique is especially important for tougher cuts, helping enhance the texture and overall eating experience.

This is a rich, low-carb take on the classic comfort dish. The recipe features tender strips of sirloin simmered with mushrooms, onions, and a creamy Greek yogurt sauce. Flavored with garlic, thyme, and Worcestershire, this take delivers a hearty, savory satisfaction without the carbs.

2 tablespoons unsalted butter

2 cups sliced white mushrooms

1 large sweet yellow onion, peeled and thinly sliced

2 cloves garlic, peeled and minced

1 pound sirloin steaks, sliced into thin strips

1 cup beef both

½ teaspoon salt

1 teaspoon Worcestershire sauce

1 tablespoon chickpea flour

1 cup plain full-fat Greek yogurt

2 tablespoons fresh thyme leaves

1. Heat butter in a large skillet over medium-high heat. Add mushrooms, onion, and garlic. Stir-fry 3 minutes or until onion is tender. Transfer to a medium bowl.
2. To the same skillet, add sirloin slices and sear 3 minutes until browned on all sides. Add broth, salt, and Worcestershire sauce. Bring to a boil. Reduce heat to low and simmer, uncovered, 7 minutes.
3. In a small bowl, make a slurry by whisking together flour and ¼ cup broth from skillet. Add slurry to skillet along with mushroom mixture, yogurt, and thyme. Stir. Lower heat to medium-low and cook, uncovered, 5 minutes. Serve warm.

Beef Soft Tacos

Loaded with smoky, spiced ground beef and topped with peppery arugula, tangy quick-pickled onions, and a zesty Greek yogurt sriracha sauce, these tacos are the best. Taco Tuesday will never be the same!

Serves 8

Per Serving

Calories	230
Fat	11g
Sodium	894mg
Carbohydrates	24g
Fiber	14g
Sugar	3g
Protein	18g

1 cup plain full-fat Greek yogurt

1 tablespoon sriracha

1 teaspoon lime juice

2 teaspoons smoked paprika

2 teaspoons chili powder

2 teaspoons onion powder

2 teaspoons garlic salt

1 tablespoon avocado oil

1 pound 80/20 ground beef

½ cup water

2 cups arugula leaves

Quick-Pickled Red Onions (Chapter 7)

8 (6-inch) low-carb flour tortillas

1. In a small bowl, create a crema by combining yogurt, sriracha, and lime juice. Refrigerate, covered, while preparing seasoning mix and beef.
2. In another small bowl, combine paprika, chili powder, and garlic salt. Set aside.
3. In a large skillet over medium-high heat, add oil. Add beef and cook 5 minutes or until browned. Drain fat. Add prepared seasoning mix and water. Bring to a boil. Reduce heat to low and simmer, uncovered, 5 minutes.
4. Assemble tacos by layering beef, arugula, yogurt crema, and Quick-Pickled Red Onions on tortillas. Fold in half to create tacos. Serve.

Philly Cheesesteak Bowls

Serves 6

Per Serving

Calories	316
Fat	19g
Sodium	521mg
Carbohydrates	5g
Fiber	1g
Sugar	2g
Protein	26g

This hearty and low-carb twist on the classic Philly cheesesteak sandwich features a mix of ground beef and pork, sautéed onion and bell peppers, and melted provolone. Each bowl is a quick, satisfying meal packed with bold flavor and cheesy goodness.

1 tablespoon avocado oil
1 small white onion, peeled and diced
1 medium green bell pepper, seeded and diced
1 medium red bell pepper, seeded and diced
1 pound 80/20 ground beef
½ pound ground pork
½ cup beef broth
1 tablespoon Worcestershire sauce
4 cloves garlic, peeled and minced
½ teaspoon salt
½ teaspoon ground black pepper
4 (1-ounce) slices provolone cheese

1. Heat avocado oil in a large skillet over medium-high heat. Add onion and bell peppers and stir-fry 2 minutes until onion is tender. Add ground beef and pork. Continue to stir-fry 4 minutes or until meat is browned.
2. Add broth, Worcestershire sauce, garlic, salt, and black pepper. Stir. Bring to a boil and reduce heat to medium-low. Simmer, uncovered, 5 minutes.
3. Top mixture with cheese. Continue to simmer, covered, 5 minutes.
4. Ladle into individual serving bowls and serve warm.

Sloppy Joe Casserole

Serves 6

Per Serving	
Calories	458
Fat	22g
Sodium	1,108mg
Carbohydrates	33g
Fiber	1g
Sugar	12g
Protein	26g

This recipe transforms the classic sandwich into a hearty oven-baked dish with a mix of seasoned ground beef and pork in a tangy tomato sauce, layered under a gluten-free corn bread. It makes for an easy, family-friendly meal that captures the sweet and savory flavors of traditional sloppy joes in a comforting casserole form.

Sloppy Joes

1 tablespoon avocado oil
1 small white onion, peeled and diced
1 medium green bell pepper, seeded and diced
1 pound 80/20 ground beef
½ pound ground pork
2 tablespoons no-sugar-added ketchup
1 (8-ounce) can tomato sauce
1 tablespoon Worcestershire sauce
4 cloves garlic, peeled and minced
1 tablespoon sriracha
1 teaspoon yellow mustard
1 teaspoon salt
1 teaspoon ground black pepper

Corn Bread Topping

1¼ cups gluten-free corn bread mix
1 large egg
½ cup grated sharp Cheddar cheese
¾ cup unsweetened almond milk

1. Preheat oven to 350°F.
2. For the sloppy joes: Add oil to a large skillet over medium-high heat. Add onion, bell pepper, beef, and pork. Sauté 5 minutes or until meat is browned.
3. Add ketchup, tomato sauce, Worcestershire sauce, garlic, sriracha, mustard, salt, and black pepper. Stir and sauté an additional 2 minutes. Add mixture to a 9" × 9" baking dish coated with nonstick cooking spray.
4. For the corn bread topping: In a medium bowl, combine all ingredients.
5. Spread corn bread topping over sloppy joes.
6. Bake 20 minutes. Remove from oven and let rest 10 minutes. Serve warm.

Mozzarella-Stuffed Meatballs

Filled with a melty mozzarella center, these meatballs are tender, juicy bites made from a flavorful blend of beef and pork seasoned with Italian herbs and Parmesan. They are pure comfort food and low carb to boot! Enjoy these in a bowl or atop a bed of zucchini noodles.

Yields 12 meatballs

Per Serving (Serving size: 1 meatball)

Calories	169
Fat	10g
Sodium	511mg
Carbohydrates	4g
Fiber	1g
Sugar	2g
Protein	14g

1 large egg white
1 tablespoon whole milk
1⁄4 cup crushed pork rinds
1⁄4 cup grated Parmesan cheese
1⁄2 pound 80/20 ground beef
1⁄2 pound ground pork
2 tablespoons grated white onion
1 teaspoon Italian seasoning
1⁄2 teaspoon salt
1⁄4 teaspoon ground black pepper
12 fresh bocconcini (mozzarella balls)
1 (23.5-ounce) jar no-sugar-added marinara sauce

1. Preheat oven to 350°F.
2. In a large bowl, whisk egg white. Add milk, pork rinds, and Parmesan cheese and combine. Add beef, pork, onion, Italian seasoning, salt, and black pepper. Combine but don't overmix. Divide into twelve equal balls.
3. Place a bocconcini in the center of each meatball and shape the meat around it, fully enclosing the cheese. Place meatballs in a cast iron pan or an ovenproof skillet. Bake 30 minutes.
4. Transfer pan to the stovetop. Pour marinara sauce over meatballs. Bring to a boil. Reduce heat to low and simmer 15 minutes. Serve warm.

Bocconcini Mozzarella Substitutions

Bocconcini are the smallest of the mozzarella balls and can usually be found in the deli section of grocery stores near the "fancy" cheeses. They generally weigh about 1 ounce each. If you cannot find this mozzarella, you can either dice a block of mozzarella or slice a mozzarella stick into four sections.

Stuffed Beefsteak Tomatoes

Serves 6

Per Serving

Calories	291
Fat	14g
Sodium	722mg
Carbohydrates	17g
Fiber	3g
Sugar	10g
Protein	21g

What Is a Beefsteak Tomato?

A beefsteak tomato is a large, juicy, and meaty variety known for its mild flavor and minimal seeds. Not only are beefsteak tomatoes perfect for slicing straight onto your plate, but they are also good for sandwiches and burgers—and for stuffing! If you need a substitute, use another large, firm variety like an heirloom or a vine-ripened tomato.

These hearty oven-baked tomatoes filled with a savory blend of ground beef, mushrooms, onion, and garlic, all seasoned with basil, Worcestershire sauce, and tomato sauce, are almost a deconstructed meatloaf in a tomato cup. Topped with melted mozzarella, they offer a flavorful, comforting meal perfect for any night of the week.

6 beefsteak tomatoes

1 tablespoon avocado oil

1 pound 80/20 ground beef

1 medium yellow onion, peeled and grated

1 cup diced white mushrooms

4 cloves garlic, peeled and minced

1 (8-ounce) can tomato sauce

1 teaspoon Worcestershire sauce

2 teaspoons dried basil

1 teaspoon salt

1 teaspoon ground black pepper

1½ cups shredded mozzarella cheese

1. Preheat oven to 375°F.
2. Cut top off each tomato. Scoop out pulp and place in a medium bowl. Set pulp aside. Add tomato cups to a 9" × 9" ungreased baking dish.
3. In a large skillet, heat oil over medium-high heat. Add beef and stir-fry 3 minutes or until almost browned. Add onion, mushrooms, and garlic. Stir-fry an additional 2 minutes. Add remaining ingredients, except mozzarella, and tomato pulp. Stir-fry an additional 4 minutes.
4. Using a slotted spoon, distribute beef mixture among tomato cups. Top with mozzarella cheese.
5. Bake 20 minutes. Let rest 10 minutes. Serve warm.

Oven Pulled Pork

This is a tender, slow-roasted dish made with seasoned pork shoulder, garlic, and gluten-free beer, creating rich flavor and juicy texture. Pulled pork is great to make in your meal prep for the week. Once you initially cook the pork, you can add barbecue sauce to a portion when heating it up during the week or add a portion to a quick Asian stir-fry for a weeknight meal.

Serves 8

Per Serving

Calories	452
Fat	29g
Sodium	539mg
Carbohydrates	1g
Fiber	0g
Sugar	0g
Protein	43g

1 tablespoon avocado oil

1 (4½-pound) pork butt/shoulder, trimmed

1 teaspoon salt

1 teaspoon ground black pepper

6 cloves garlic, peeled and halved

1 cup gluten-free beer

1. Preheat oven to 300°F. Line a 13" × 9" baking dish with aluminum foil.
2. Rub oil over pork and season on all sides with salt and black pepper. Place in baking dish. Scatter garlic cloves around the pork for aromatics. Pour in beer. Cover with aluminum foil.
3. Bake 3½ hours. Remove foil and let rest 10 minutes.
4. Using two forks, pull meat apart. Serve warm.

Thai Burger Patties with Quick-Pickled Vegetables

Here, juicy, flavor-packed patties pair with crisp and tangy pickled vegetables, offering a perfect balance of savory, spicy, and refreshing flavors. Serve as is, on a low-carb bun, or with a scoop of cauliflower rice.

Serves 6

Per Serving

Calories	338
Fat	19g
Sodium	1,162mg
Carbohydrates	8g
Fiber	1g
Sugar	5g
Protein	31g

Quick-Pickled Vegetables

- ½ cup hot water
- 1 teaspoon salt
- 1 tablespoon agave nectar
- ½ cup white vinegar
- 1 cup shredded carrots
- 1 cup thinly sliced, half-moon-shaped English cucumber slices
- 1 medium jalapeño, seeded and thinly sliced

Thai Burger Patties

- 1 pound ground pork
- 1 pound ground turkey
- 1 small yellow onion, peeled and grated
- 2 teaspoons salt
- 1 teaspoon cayenne pepper
- 1 teaspoon garlic powder
- 1 tablespoon fish sauce
- 1 tablespoon honey
- 1 tablespoon dried cilantro
- 2 tablespoons avocado oil

1. For the quick-pickled vegetables: In a medium bowl, combine hot water and salt and stir until salt is dissolved. Stir in agave nectar and vinegar. Add carrots, cucumber, and jalapeño. Refrigerate, covered, 1 hour.
2. For the Thai burger patties: In a large bowl, combine pork, turkey, onion, salt, cayenne pepper, garlic powder, fish sauce, honey, and cilantro. Form into six equal balls.
3. Heat oil in a large skillet over medium-high heat. Place balls in skillet and press down on each one to form patties. Cook 4 minutes on each side or until the internal temperature reaches 160°F. Transfer patties to a serving plate and let rest 5 minutes.
4. Serve warm with quick-pickled vegetables on top.

What Else Can You Quick-Pickle?

Use the basic pickling method in this recipe on red onions, radishes, or whatever is in season. You can add peppercorns or fresh herbs as well. These pickled vegetables are not only good on burgers, but they also perk up breakfast eggs, protein bowls, salads, or most anything!

Pork Egg Roll Bowl

Serves 4	
Per Serving	
Calories	408
Fat	17g
Sodium	696mg
Carbohydrates	33g
Fiber	10g
Sugar	17g
Protein	26g

Who needs the carb wrapper when all the goodness is on the inside of the egg roll? This is a perfect prep day recipe. Double it and refrigerate up to 5 days so you can have several flavor-filled lunches and dinners for you and your family.

1 tablespoon sesame oil

1 pound ground pork

8 ounces shiitake mushrooms

2 green onions, sliced (white and green parts separated)

1 cup shredded carrots

1 (14-ounce) bag coleslaw mix

1 (1-inch) piece fresh ginger, grated

¼ cup coconut aminos

1 teaspoon fish sauce

1 tablespoon sriracha

1 teaspoon apple cider vinegar

2 teaspoons honey

4 cloves garlic, peeled and minced

1. In a large skillet over medium-high heat, add oil and ground pork. Stir fry 4 minutes or until almost done. Push meat to the side and add mushrooms, whites of green onions, and carrots. Stir-fry 3 minutes or until vegetables are tender. Stir pork in with vegetables.
2. Add coleslaw mix, ginger, coconut aminos, fish sauce, sriracha, vinegar, honey, and garlic. Cover and simmer 5 minutes or until coleslaw mix is steamed and reduced. Stir ingredients together.
3. Spoon into individual serving bowls. Garnish with greens of green onions and serve warm.

Roasted Pork Tenderloin

Roasting a pork tenderloin correctly can yield a juicy and tender loin. Using your meat thermometer can help control overcooking and is particularly necessary with a tenderloin. Enjoy this with a scoop of Summer Squash Casserole (Chapter 7).

Serves 8

Per Serving

Calories	238
Fat	7g
Sodium	822mg
Carbohydrates	1g
Fiber	0g
Sugar	0g
Protein	41g

1 (4-pound) package boneless pork tenderloins

2 tablespoons Dijon mustard

1 teaspoon salt

1 teaspoon ground black pepper

1. Preheat oven to 350°F. Spray a large casserole dish with nonstick cooking spray.
2. Add tenderloins to dish. Brush mustard over loins. Season with salt and black pepper.
3. Bake 20 minutes. Flip loins and bake an additional 20 minutes or until internal temperature reaches 145°F.
4. Let rest 10 minutes, slice, and serve warm.

Skillet Pork Chops with Plums

Serves 4

Per Serving

Calories	439
Fat	14g
Sodium	893mg
Carbohydrates	20g
Fiber	3g
Sugar	14g
Protein	44g

Plum Substitutions

Pineapple and peaches are delicious alternatives to plums in this recipe. Depending on how ripe the peaches are, you may need to cook them only 3 minutes before returning the pork chops to the skillet.

This savory-sweet dish pairs juicy, spice-rubbed pork chops with sweet plums and red onion. Finished with fresh thyme and a splash of coconut aminos, it's a vibrant dish full of bold flavor. Accompany this one-pan wonder with a simple green salad.

1 teaspoon salt

1 teaspoon ground black pepper

1 teaspoon smoked paprika

1 teaspoon ground yellow mustard

1 teaspoon garlic powder

4 (7-ounce, 1-inch-thick) bone-in pork chops

1 tablespoon avocado oil

1 small red onion, peeled and sliced

8 medium plums, halved and pitted

2 tablespoons coconut aminos

1 tablespoon fresh thyme leaves

1 tablespoon water

1. In a small bowl, combine salt, black pepper, paprika, mustard, and garlic powder. Season pork chops with mixture.
2. In a cast iron skillet, heat oil over high heat. Sear pork chops 1 minute on each side. Set aside.
3. To the skillet, add red onion, plums, coconut aminos, and thyme. Stir-fry 5 minutes or until plums are browned and onions are tender. Return pork chops to skillet. Add water. Reduce heat to low and simmer, covered, 15 minutes or until internal temperature of pork chops reaches 160°F.
4. Let rest 10 minutes. Serve warm.

Mushroom and Swiss-Stuffed Pork Chops

There are some classic combos like peanut butter and jelly, pizza and beer, and, well, mushrooms and Swiss cheese. Take it up a notch by stuffing that particular combo into salty, tender pork chops for a decadent meal that will put smiles on the faces of everyone at the table!

Serves 4

Per Serving

Calories	598
Fat	34g
Sodium	830mg
Carbohydrates	4g
Fiber	1g
Sugar	2g
Protein	49g

4 ounces cream cheese, room temperature

½ cup grated Swiss cheese

2 tablespoons avocado oil, divided

2 cups chopped white mushrooms

¼ cup grated yellow onion

1 cup chopped baby spinach

4 (7-ounce, 1-inch-thick) bone-in pork chops

1 teaspoon salt

½ teaspoon ground black pepper

3 tablespoons unsalted butter

1. Preheat oven to 350°F.
2. In a large bowl, combine cream cheese and Swiss cheese.
3. In a large ovenproof skillet, heat 1 tablespoon oil over medium-high heat. Add mushrooms, onion, and spinach and cook 3 minutes. Remove from heat and add to bowl with cheese. Stir.
4. Cut a slit in each pork chop. Move the knife back and forth from front to back. The initial incision should be no larger than the width of the knife. Stuff cheese mixture into each pork chop. Season with salt and black pepper.
5. Add remaining oil to the same skillet and set over high heat. Add pork chops and sear 2 minutes per side. Add butter. Move skillet to oven and bake 12 minutes or until pork reaches an internal temperature of 145°F.
6. Let rest 7 minutes. Serve warm.

Baked Baby Back Pork Ribs

Serves 4

Per Serving

Calories	558
Fat	38g
Sodium	1,524mg
Carbohydrates	4g
Fiber	1g
Sugar	0g
Protein	46g

Soy Sauce Substitutes

Coconut aminos are an excellent umami substitute for soy sauce. They are a soy-free alternative made from coconut tree sap and salt. Tamari is a gluten-free substitute that is a little deeper in flavor than coconut aminos. Both are viable twins to soy sauce; use what fits best with your dietary needs.

It can sometimes be hard to find barbecue sauces without added sugar, but there's no need to worry. You can achieve full flavor and fall-off-the-bone ribs with this aluminum foil baking process using simple pantry staples to achieve deliciousness!

2 tablespoons avocado oil

1 tablespoon coconut aminos

1 tablespoon Dijon mustard

1 (2-pound) rack baby back pork ribs

2 teaspoons salt

1 teaspoon ground black pepper

1 teaspoon cayenne pepper

1 teaspoon cocoa powder

2 teaspoons smoked paprika

2 teaspoons ground espresso powder

1. Preheat oven to 350°F.
2. In a small bowl, whisk together oil, coconut aminos, and mustard. Brush entire top, bottom, and sides of ribs with mixture.
3. In another small bowl, combine salt, black pepper, cayenne pepper, cocoa powder, paprika, and espresso powder. Massage into ribs.
4. Wrap and seal ribs in aluminum foil. Place on an ungreased rimmed baking sheet. Bake 3 hours.
5. Remove foil and serve warm.

Garlic Basil Frenched Rack of Lamb

Serves 2

Per Serving

Calories	1,114
Fat	89g
Sodium	1,707mg
Carbohydrates	6g
Fiber	0g
Sugar	3g
Protein	55g

What Is a "Frenched" Rack of Lamb?

A "frenched" rack of lamb refers to a rack that has had the meat and fat carefully trimmed away from the ends of the rib bones, leaving them exposed for a more elegant and refined presentation. This technique is typically used for visual appeal and to make the rack easier to handle, carve, and serve.

This high-protein recipe features tender lamb racks marinated in a blend of avocado oil, horseradish mustard, garlic, and fresh basil and then roasted to a juicy, flavorful finish. The frenched bones create a beautiful presentation, making this dish perfect for special occasions or elegant dinners.

¼ cup avocado oil

2 tablespoons horseradish mustard

1 teaspoon salt

6 cloves garlic, peeled

¼ cup basil leaves

Bone-in frenched rack of lamb, 8 ribs connected

1. Preheat oven to 450°F. Line a baking sheet with parchment paper.
2. In a food processor, add oil, horseradish mustard, salt, garlic, and basil and pulse into a paste. Massage paste into ribs.
3. Place ribs, fat side up, on baking sheet.
4. Bake 25 minutes or until internal temperature reaches 130°F. Remove from oven and let rest 10 minutes.
5. Slice between rib bones and serve warm.

Lamb Burgers

These rich, juicy, and aromatic burgers are sure to excite your taste buds. Whether you are making them as a high-protein dinner for your family or doubling the recipe for a backyard cookout, everyone will welcome these Greek-inspired patties! You can eat these burgers as is, in a lettuce wrap, or even on a low-carb bun. If you want to kick things up a notch, add arugula and a thinly sliced red onion.

Serves 6

Per Serving

Calories	420
Fat	29g
Sodium	906mg
Carbohydrates	2g
Fiber	1g
Sugar	1g
Protein	32g

2 pounds ground lamb

1 teaspoon garlic powder

2 teaspoons salt

2 teaspoons smoked paprika

2 teaspoons cumin

⅛ teaspoon ground cinnamon

1 teaspoon dried dill

1 teaspoon dried mint

2 tablespoons avocado oil

½ cup Tzatziki Sauce (Chapter 9)

1. In a large bowl, combine lamb, garlic powder, salt, paprika, cumin, cinnamon, dill, and mint. Form into six equal balls.
2. Heat oil in a large skillet over medium-high heat. Place balls in skillet and press down on each one to form patties. Cook 3 minutes on each side or until the internal temperature reaches 135°F.
3. Transfer patties to a serving plate and let rest 5 minutes.
4. Serve warm with Tzatziki Sauce drizzled over patties.

CHAPTER 6

Fish and Seafood

Crusted Chili Lime Cod ... 126
Baked Fish Sticks ... 127
Cast Iron Cod and Ratatouille-Style Vegetables ... 129
Salmon Patties with Sriracha Lime Crema ... 130
Snow Crab Legs with Chili Mustard Butter ... 131
Curried Coconut Shrimp ... 132
Butter Shrimp ... 133
Parmesan Flounder ... 133
Pan-Seared Salmon ... 135
Thai Peanut "Noodles" with Shrimp ... 136
BBQ Shrimp ... 137
Sea Bass in Parchment (en Papillote) ... 138
Baked Tilapia ... 139
Creamy Hearts of Palm Linguini with Shrimp ... 140
Pecan-Crusted Barramundi ... 142
Caper and Lemon Butter Halibut ... 143
Mexican Mussels ... 144
Lobster Lettuce Wraps ... 145
Fish Tacos ... 147
Steamed Littleneck Clams ... 148
Steamed Lobster Tails ... 149
Baked Crab Cakes ... 150

Crusted Chili Lime Cod

Serves 2

Per Serving

Calories	254
Fat	9g
Sodium	395mg
Carbohydrates	1g
Fiber	0g
Sugar	0g
Protein	35g

Alternative Ways to Do Crushed Pork Rinds

Although traditional pork rinds are found at most grocery store chains, some chains carry flavored pork rinds, which can add another level of flavor to your recipe. Pre-crushed rinds in the form of "pork panko" are also available.

Here, crushed pork rinds, or pork panko, replace high-carb bread crumbs. The pork rinds lend their crunchiness to the cod but leave the carbs out. You can find them at most supermarkets in different flavors or even already crushed.

½ cup crushed pork rinds
⅛ teaspoon cayenne pepper
1 tablespoon Dijon mustard
1 teaspoon lime juice
1 tablespoon unsalted butter, melted
2 (6-ounce) cod fillets

1. Preheat oven to 350°F. Line a baking sheet with parchment paper.
2. In a small bowl, combine pork rinds, cayenne pepper, mustard, lime juice, and butter.
3. Press mixture across tops of cod fillets. Place on baking sheet.
4. Bake 20 minutes or until fish is opaque and flaky. Serve warm.

Baked Fish Sticks

These fish sticks are coated in pork panko and Parmesan and come out crispy and golden without the need for deep frying, offering a low-carb twist on a classic comfort food. Use them in Fish Tacos (see recipe in this chapter) or just dip them in some Blueberry Ketchup (Chapter 9).

Serves 4

Per Serving

Calories	309
Fat	17g
Sodium	202mg
Carbohydrates	4g
Fiber	2g
Sugar	1g
Protein	32g

1 cup almond flour

2 large eggs

1 cup pork panko

½ cup grated Parmesan cheese

½ teaspoon ground black pepper

1 pound cod fillets, sliced into ½-inch-wide sticks

1. Preheat oven to 350°F. Line a baking sheet with parchment paper.
2. In one medium bowl, add almond flour. In a second medium bowl, whisk eggs. In a third medium bowl, combine pork panko, Parmesan cheese, and black pepper.
3. Dip a fish stick in almond flour, shaking off any excess. Dredge fish in eggs, shaking off any excess. Roll fish in panko mixture. Place on baking sheet. Repeat with remaining fish sticks.
4. Bake 20 minutes or until browned. Serve warm.

Pork Panko Substitutions

If for some reason you cannot have, or simply do not like, pork panko, you can use a variety of other items as breading on these fish sticks such as crushed pretzels, potato chips, oats, your favorite nuts or seeds, or even coconut.

Cast Iron Cod and Ratatouille-Style Vegetables

Featuring flaky and pan-seared cod fillets nestled in a medley of sautéed zucchini, yellow summer squash, eggplant, bell pepper, onion, and tomatoes, this dish is cooked to perfection in a cast iron skillet. The fish adds protein, while the medley of vegetables lends healthy carbs to a filling meal.

Serves 4

Per Serving

Calories	289
Fat	11g
Sodium	681mg
Carbohydrates	13g
Fiber	4g
Sugar	7g
Protein	33g

3 tablespoons avocado oil, divided

4 (6-ounce) cod fillets

1 medium zucchini, diced

1 medium yellow summer squash, diced

½ large eggplant, peeled and diced

1 large orange bell pepper, seeded and sliced

1 medium yellow onion, peeled and diced

4 cloves garlic, peeled and minced

1 teaspoon salt

⅛ teaspoon cayenne pepper

1 (28-ounce) canned diced tomatoes, including juice

2 tablespoons chopped chives

1. In a cast iron skillet, heat 1 tablespoon oil over medium-high heat. Add cod and sear fillets 2 minutes on each side. Transfer to a plate.
2. In the same skillet, add remaining oil. Add zucchini, yellow squash, eggplant, bell pepper, onion, and garlic. Sauté 3 minutes or until onion is tender.
3. Stir in salt, cayenne pepper, and tomatoes and juice. Heat 2–3 minutes until mixture is warmed. Nestle cod fillets into vegetable mixture. Cover and simmer 5 minutes or until cod is cooked through.
4. Serve warm garnished with chives.

Salmon Patties with Sriracha Lime Crema

Serves 4

Per Serving

Calories	349
Fat	19g
Sodium	831mg
Carbohydrates	4g
Fiber	0g
Sugar	3g
Protein	37g

These low-carb golden and crispy patties made from flaked salmon, herbs, and pork panko are pan-fried to perfection. They're topped with a spicy yogurt-based crema made from lime juice and sriracha, adding a bold kick to every bite.

1 cup plain full-fat Greek yogurt
2 teaspoons sriracha
2 teaspoons lime juice
⅛ teaspoon salt
1 teaspoon water
1 (14.75-ounce) can salmon
2 large eggs, whisked
¼ cup pork panko
2 tablespoons mayonnaise
1 teaspoon prepared horseradish
1 teaspoon dried dill
¼ teaspoon salt
¼ teaspoon ground black pepper
1 tablespoon avocado oil
1 tablespoon capers, drained

1. In a small bowl, combine yogurt, sriracha, lime juice, and salt to form a crema. Add water a little at a time until crema is of drizzling consistency. Refrigerate, covered, until ready to use.
2. In a medium bowl, combine salmon, eggs, pork panko, mayonnaise, horseradish, dill, salt, and black pepper.
3. In a large skillet, heat oil over medium-high heat. Scoop ¼ cup salmon mixture onto skillet. Repeat with remaining mixture. Using a spatula, gently press on each scoop to form patties. Cook on each side 3 minutes or until patties are browned and cooked through.
4. Plate warm patties. Drizzle with crema and garnish with capers. Serve.

Snow Crab Legs with Chili Mustard Butter

Naturally low-carb crab legs are both elegant and easy to prepare. The rich, melted butter is infused with Dijon mustard, chili powder, and shallot, adding a zesty kick to the naturally sweet crabmeat. Perfect for a special dinner, this high-protein dish is simple yet indulgent.

Serves 2

Per Serving

Calories	561
Fat	45g
Sodium	1,160mg
Carbohydrates	3g
Fiber	1g
Sugar	1g
Protein	29g

2 pounds frozen snow crab legs, thawed

1 stick unsalted butter

1 medium shallot, peeled and diced

1 tablespoon Dijon mustard

1 teaspoon lemon juice

1 teaspoon chili powder

1⁄8 teaspoon salt

1. In a large pot, add crab legs. Add enough water to cover legs. Bring to a boil. Reduce heat to low and simmer, covered, 5 minutes. Remove legs.
2. In a small saucepan over medium heat, add butter and shallot. Cook 2 minutes or until shallot is tender. Add remaining ingredients. Stir to combine.
3. Serve crab legs with flavored butter for dipping.

Curried Coconut Shrimp

Serves 4

Per Serving

Calories	268
Fat	18g
Sodium	1,296mg
Carbohydrates	8g
Fiber	1g
Sugar	4g
Protein	17g

This bold and creamy dish features tender shrimp simmered in a spiced coconut tomato sauce. Infused with curry, cumin, and just a hint of sweetness from honey, it's a flavorful, low-carb meal that comes together quickly. High in protein and full of aromatic spices, it's perfect for a weeknight dinner that feels anything but ordinary.

1 teaspoon curry powder

1 teaspoon salt

½ teaspoon garlic powder

¼ teaspoon cayenne powder

1 pound large raw shrimp, peeled, deveined, tails removed

2 tablespoons unsalted butter

1 cup canned coconut milk

2 tablespoons tomato paste

2 teaspoons honey

2 teaspoons cumin

½ teaspoon ground ginger

½ teaspoon cayenne pepper

2 tablespoons chopped fresh cilantro

1. In a medium bowl, combine curry powder, salt, garlic powder, and cayenne powder. Add shrimp and toss to coat.
2. In a large skillet, heat butter over medium-high heat. Add shrimp and cook 3 minutes, flipping shrimp until no longer opaque. Transfer shrimp to a plate.
3. In the same skillet, whisk together coconut milk, tomato paste, honey, cumin, ginger, and cayenne pepper. Bring to a boil. Reduce heat to low. Return shrimp to skillet. Simmer, uncovered, 7 minutes. Remove from heat.
4. Ladle into individual serving bowls, garnish with cilantro, and serve warm.

Butter Shrimp

Serves 4	
Per Serving	
Calories	184
Fat	12g
Sodium	734mg
Carbohydrates	2g
Fiber	0g
Sugar	0g
Protein	16g

This dish is so easy to make that it can be enjoyed several times a week with little prep or cook time. Naturally low in carbs and high in protein, it's perfect served on its own, over cauliflower rice, or alongside roasted vegetables.

¼ cup salted butter

1 pound large raw shrimp, peeled, deveined, tails removed

2 tablespoons lemon juice

¼ cup fresh parsley leaves

1. In a large skillet, melt butter over medium-high heat. Add shrimp and cook approximately 5 minutes, flipping shrimp, until no longer opaque and cooked through.
2. Remove from heat and stir in lemon juice. Transfer to individual serving bowls and garnish with parsley. Serve warm.

Parmesan Flounder

Serves 4	
Per Serving	
Calories	309
Fat	16g
Sodium	900mg
Carbohydrates	0g
Fiber	0g
Sugar	0g
Protein	34g

This alternative to deep-fried fish features a flavorful mix of Parmesan and crushed pork rinds. Baked to a golden, crunchy finish, this flounder delivers big flavor without the carbs.

4 flounder fillets (2 pounds total weight)

½ cup grated Parmesan cheese

½ cup crushed pork rinds

¼ teaspoon ground black pepper

4 tablespoons unsalted butter, melted

1. Preheat oven to 425°F. Line a 9" × 13" baking dish with parchment paper.
2. Add flounder to baking dish.
3. In a small bowl, stir together Parmesan cheese, pork rinds, black pepper, and butter. Press mixture on top of each fillet.
4. Bake 12 minutes. Let rest 5 minutes. Transfer to plates and serve warm.

Pan-Seared Salmon

A crisp skin and flaky interior are achieved by quickly cooking the salmon fillets in a hot skillet. The minimal ingredients in this simple, elegant dish highlight the rich flavor of the salmon. Serve with or on a fresh salad or with roasted asparagus.

Serves 4

Per Serving

Calories	420
Fat	24g
Sodium	433mg
Carbohydrates	1g
Fiber	0g
Sugar	0g
Protein	35g

2 tablespoons Dijon mustard
2 teaspoons chopped fresh dill
2 teaspoons lemon juice
½ teaspoon grated lemon zest
¼ teaspoon salt
3 tablespoons melted unsalted butter, divided
4 (6-ounce) salmon fillets
½ medium lemon, cut into 4 wedges

1. In a small bowl, whisk together mustard, dill, lemon juice, lemon zest, salt, and 1 tablespoon butter.
2. In a large skillet over medium-high heat, heat remaining butter. Add salmon, skin side down, to skillet. Brush prepared sauce over fillets. Cook 6 minutes. Flip fillets and finish cooking 1 additional minute, brushing sauce from skillet over fillets while cooking.
3. Transfer to plates, skin side up, and let rest 5 minutes. Squeeze a lemon wedge over each fillet. Serve warm.

Your Salmon Fillets Are Different Sizes!

When cooking fish, the fillets are often different sizes. Some are thick, while others are thin. And some are both in the same fillet. This recipe offers a simple guideline, but to avoid overcooking, just make sure that each fillet reaches an internal temperature of 130°F. To ensure even doneness, consider starting with thicker fillets or removing thinner ones earlier during pan-searing, baking, or grilling.

Thai Peanut "Noodles" with Shrimp

Serves 6

Per Serving

Calories	261
Fat	9g
Sodium	808mg
Carbohydrates	26g
Fiber	8g
Sugar	10g
Protein	17g

Take this low-carb dish to the next level by garnishing it with crushed peanuts and fresh cilantro (or parsley!) leaves.

¼ cup creamy no-sugar-added peanut butter
¼ cup coconut aminos
4 cloves garlic, peeled and minced
1 tablespoon honey
1 tablespoon apple cider vinegar
1 teaspoon sesame oil
1 teaspoon sriracha
1 tablespoon avocado oil
1 pound medium shrimp, peeled, deveined, tails removed
1 (14-ounce) bag coleslaw mix
2 (12-ounce) packets hearts of palm linguini, drained

1. In a medium bowl, whisk together peanut butter, coconut aminos, garlic, honey, vinegar, sesame oil, and sriracha. Set aside.
2. In a large skillet, heat avocado oil over medium heat. Add shrimp and stir-fry 2 minutes or until shrimp is mostly cooked.
3. Add coleslaw and stir-fry 2 minutes. Add linguini and stir-fry an additional 2 minutes. Add peanut butter mixture and stir-fry 4 minutes or until everything is warmed through.
4. Transfer to individual serving bowls and serve warm.

BBQ Shrimp

BBQ shrimp make a great appetizer or a high-protein meal. If you don't want to use an indoor grilling pan, this is a perfect meal to throw on your outdoor grill! Also, experiment with the many no-sugar-added barbecue sauces on the market. From traditional to mesquite, there are many options to choose from.

Serves 6	
Per Serving	
Calories	141
Fat	4g
Sodium	912mg
Carbohydrates	2g
Fiber	0g
Sugar	0g
Protein	21g

2 pounds medium raw shrimp, peeled and deveined

¼ cup no-sugar-added barbecue sauce, divided

2 tablespoons avocado oil, divided

1. Soak wooden skewers in water 30 minutes.
2. Place shrimp in a medium bowl and add half of barbecue sauce. Toss to coat. Add 4 shrimp to each wooden skewer.
3. In large grill pan, add 1 tablespoon oil and set over medium-high heat. Add half of the skewers. Grill 2 minutes. Flip and brush some barbecue sauce over shrimp. Grill 2 minutes. Flip and brush more barbecue sauce over shrimp. Grill an additional minute. Repeat with remaining oil and skewers.
4. Transfer skewers to a serving plate and serve warm.

Sea Bass in Parchment (en Papillote)

Serves 2

Per Serving

Calories	295
Fat	11g
Sodium	548mg
Carbohydrates	8g
Fiber	2g
Sugar	6g
Protein	38g

Creating Parchment Paper Pockets (En Papillote)

To create a parchment paper pocket, cut a large heart shape from a sheet of parchment paper, place your ingredients on one half, fold over, and tightly crimp the edges to seal. If you would like a visual of this, the Internet is full of how-to videos.

This high-protein, low-carb meal is elegant yet easy—perfect for a healthy weeknight dinner or for entertaining. And if you really want to create a special moment, let your guests open their parchment pocket. It is like a little present and makes for a fun presentation.

½ cup plain full-fat Greek yogurt
1 tablespoon lemon juice
1 tablespoon chopped fresh dill
1 teaspoon berbere seasoning
2 (6-ounce) sea bass fillets
6 cherry tomatoes
10 pitted kalamata olives, halved
1 small zucchini, sliced

1. Preheat oven to 400°F. Prepare two sheets of parchment paper (see sidebar).
2. In a small bowl, combine yogurt, lemon juice, dill, and berbere seasoning.
3. Place each sea bass fillet on one half of its own parchment paper. Spread yogurt mixture over fillets. Scatter tomatoes, olives, and zucchini around each fillet. Seal parchment paper pockets and place in a 9" × 13" ungreased baking dish.
4. Bake 20 minutes. Let rest 5 minutes. Open up parchment pockets and serve warm.

Baked Tilapia

Tilapia is a thin fillet, making this protein-packed dish easy to prep and ready in minutes on those busy nights. Garnish with fresh parsley leaves for an added touch.

Serves 4

Per Serving

Calories	241
Fat	10g
Sodium	646mg
Carbohydrates	1g
Fiber	0g
Sugar	0g
Protein	34g

3 tablespoons salted butter, melted

2 tablespoons lemon juice

1 teaspoon garlic salt

1 teaspoon Italian seasoning

4 (6-ounce) tilapia fillets

1. Preheat oven to 400°F.
2. In a small bowl, combine butter, lemon juice, garlic salt, and Italian seasoning.
3. Place tilapia in a 9" × 13" ungreased baking dish. Pour butter mixture over tilapia.
4. Bake 10 minutes. Let rest 5 minutes. Serve warm.

Creamy Hearts of Palm Linguini with Shrimp

Serves 6

Per Serving

Calories	141
Fat	4g
Sodium	852mg
Carbohydrates	8g
Fiber	3g
Sugar	1g
Protein	16g

This recipe is a low-carb "pasta" dish made with tender hearts of palm noodles tossed with a simple sour cream–based sauce. Juicy sautéed shrimp add protein and flavor, making for a satisfying and elegant meal.

1 tablespoon avocado oil

1 pound medium shrimp, peeled, deveined, tails removed

2 (12-ounce) packets hearts of palm linguini, drained

½ cup plain full-fat Greek yogurt

¼ cup plus 1 tablespoon grated Parmesan cheese, divided

2 tablespoons unsweetened almond milk

½ teaspoon salt

½ cup chopped fresh parsley

1 small lemon, cut into 6 wedges

1. In a large skillet, heat oil over medium heat. Add shrimp and stir-fry 4 minutes or until shrimp is opaque.
2. Toss in linguini and continue to stir-fry 1 minute. Add yogurt, ¼ cup Parmesan, almond milk, and salt. Continue stir-frying 1–2 minutes until sauce is smooth. Remove from heat and allow to rest 2 minutes.
3. Transfer to individual serving bowls and garnish with parsley, a squeeze of lemon, and remaining Parmesan. Serve warm.

Pecan-Crusted Barramundi

Serves 4

Per Serving

Calories	367
Fat	24g
Sodium	112mg
Carbohydrates	2g
Fiber	1g
Sugar	1g
Protein	35g

If you've been missing a fried fish dinner, this pecan and pork rind topping offers the same mouthfeel as a high-carb batter by creating a crunchy coating. This nutrient-dense main course has a bright, gourmet flavor.

4 (6-ounce) barramundi fillets

1 large lime, cut into 8 slices

½ cup ground pecans

½ cup crushed pork rinds

¼ teaspoon smoked paprika

1 teaspoon dried basil

4 tablespoons unsalted butter, melted

1. Preheat oven to 375°F. Line a 9" × 13" baking dish with parchment paper.
2. Add barramundi to baking dish. Place 2 lime slices under each fillet.
3. In a small bowl, stir together pecans, pork rinds, paprika, basil, and butter. Press mixture on top of each fillet.
4. Bake 12 minutes. Let rest 5 minutes. Transfer to plates and serve warm.

Caper and Lemon Butter Halibut

Enjoy this meal any night of the week, just for the halibut! But seriously, halibut is a beautiful white flaky fish that is mild enough to take on whatever flavors you add to it.

Serves 4

Per Serving

Calories	259
Fat	13g
Sodium	799mg
Carbohydrates	1g
Fiber	0g
Sugar	0g
Protein	32g

4 (6-ounce) halibut fillets

1 teaspoon salt

½ teaspoon ground black pepper

4 tablespoons unsalted butter, melted

1 teaspoon lemon zest

Juice from 1 medium lemon

2 tablespoons capers, drained

1. Preheat oven to 425°F. Line a 9" × 13" baking dish with parchment paper.
2. Add halibut fillets to baking dish. Pat fillets dry with paper towels. Season with salt and black pepper.
3. In a small bowl, combine butter, lemon zest, and lemon juice. Pour over halibut fillets. Add capers.
4. Bake 10 minutes. Transfer halibut fillets to plates and serve warm, spooning lemon butter and cooked capers over fillets.

Mexican Mussels

Serves 2

Per Serving

Calories	776
Fat	56g
Sodium	2,475mg
Carbohydrates	23g
Fiber	2g
Sugar	8g
Protein	32g

Debearding Mussels

Most grocers will sell their mussels already debearded. If this isn't the case when you buy yours, it is a fairly easy process to eliminate the fibers—it's like pulling weeds. Under running water, grab the "beard" and pull toward the hinge end of the shell. Give the mussels a good rinse to eliminate sand and impurities.

Serve this tasty high-protein dish alongside an empty bowl. As you eat your mussels, discard the shells in the bowl. At the end, you'll be left with an aromatic and deep-tasting bowl of creamy soup.

2 tablespoons unsalted butter

1 medium white onion, peeled and diced

2 cups fresh baby spinach

1 teaspoon salt

½ teaspoon ground cumin

½ teaspoon garlic powder

½ teaspoon chili powder

¼ teaspoon crushed red pepper

1 cup heavy cream

2 cups vegetable broth

1 (16-ounce) bottle gluten-free beer

2 pounds fresh mussels, debearded

¼ cup chopped fresh cilantro

1. In a Dutch oven or large pot, melt butter over medium heat. Add onion. Cook 2 minutes or until onion is tender. Add spinach, salt, cumin, garlic powder, chili powder, and crushed red pepper. Stir.
2. Add cream, broth, and gluten-free beer. Stir.
3. Add mussels to mixture. Cover pot. Raise heat to medium-high and cook 6 minutes.
4. Distribute mussels between individual serving bowls, discarding unopened ones, and distribute liquid from pot. Garnish with cilantro. Serve immediately.

Lobster Lettuce Wraps

You don't have to travel to Maine to get a "Lobsta" Roll—this bunless version has all the flavors of the original!

Serves 4

Per Serving

Calories	89
Fat	3g
Sodium	447mg
Carbohydrates	2g
Fiber	1g
Sugar	1g
Protein	12g

4 (4-ounce) lobster tails

1 cup water

1 large shallot, peeled and diced

1 tablespoon mayonnaise

2 tablespoons plain full-fat Greek yogurt

2 teaspoons lemon juice

½ teaspoon lemon zest

¼ teaspoon salt

¼ teaspoon ground black pepper

1 medium head butter lettuce, leaves separated

1. Using kitchen shears, cut the underneath cartilage of each lobster tail about halfway down. (This will allow the tails to expand during the steaming process.)
2. In a large saucepan, add water. Insert steamer basket and add lobster tails. Bring to a boil. Cover and let steam 7 minutes. When lobster tails are cool enough to handle, remove meat and chop. Add to a medium bowl. Discard shells.
3. To the same medium bowl, add shallot, mayonnaise, yogurt, lemon juice, lemon zest, salt, and black pepper.
4. Serve immediately with lettuce leaves as wraps or store refrigerated, covered, up to 3 days until ready to eat.

Fish Tacos

These tacos feature tender baked cod wrapped in low-carb tortillas, making them a healthier option than traditional fish tacos. They're topped with a fresh, vibrant peach and sweet pepper salsa and drizzled with a soothing yet kickin' crema.

Serves 8

Per Serving

Calories	426
Fat	31g
Sodium	727mg
Carbohydrates	25g
Fiber	15g
Sugar	3g
Protein	22g

Baked Fish Sticks (see recipe in this chapter)

1 cup mayonnaise

2 teaspoons sriracha

2 teaspoons fresh lime juice

8 (6-inch) low-carb flour tortillas

1½ cups Peach and Sweet Pepper Salsa (Chapter 9)

1. Prepare Baked Fish Sticks.
2. In a small bowl, whisk together mayonnaise, sriracha, and lime juice to form a crema.
3. Distribute fish sticks among middle of tortillas. Drizzle with sriracha lime crema. Fold in half to create a taco. Garnish with Peach and Sweet Pepper Salsa. Serve.

Add More Crunch to Your Tacos

For some added crunch in these tacos, buy a 16-ounce bag of pre-shredded coleslaw mix. Add 2 tablespoons mayonnaise and 2 tablespoons apple cider vinegar to the mix. Season with salt and ground black pepper to taste. Add a little of this slaw to your Fish Tacos for a delicious crunch.

Steamed Littleneck Clams

Serves 2

Per Serving

Calories	284
Fat	22g
Sodium	766mg
Carbohydrates	4g
Fiber	0g
Sugar	0g
Protein	14g

Also referred to as bay cockles or rock cockles, littleneck clams are the smallest of the hard-shell clams seen on menus or in stores. Though little in size, they are big in flavor, so you won't regret giving these clams a try.

2 pounds littleneck clams (approximately 20)

1 cup vegetable broth

¼ cup chopped fresh parsley

1 medium lemon, quartered

¼ cup salted butter, melted

1. Rinse clams under cold water to remove any grit from shells. Discard any broken shells.
2. In a large pot, add clams and broth. Bring to a boil. Cover and let steam 7 minutes or until clams have opened. Transfer clams to a serving bowl. Discard any that did not open.
3. Garnish with parsley and lemon quarters. Serve warm with melted butter on the side.

Steamed Lobster Tails

You don't have to wait for a special occasion to enjoy lobster tails. Not only do they fit right into a low-carb, high-protein diet, but they are so easy to cook. So, pour yourself a glass of chardonnay and enjoy a fancy meal.

Serves 2

Per Serving

Calories	515
Fat	44g
Sodium	1,288mg
Carbohydrates	2g
Fiber	0g
Sugar	1g
Protein	22g

4 (4-ounce) lobster tails

½ cup salted butter (1 stick)

¾ cup vegetable broth

2 cloves garlic, peeled and minced

¼ teaspoon Old Bay Seasoning

2 tablespoons chopped fresh parsley leaves

1. Using kitchen shears, cut the underneath cartilage of each lobster tail about halfway down. (This will allow the tails to expand during the steaming process.)
2. In a large saucepan, add butter, broth, garlic, Old Bay, and parsley. Insert steamer basket and add lobster tails.
3. Bring to a boil. Cover and let steam 7 minutes.
4. Transfer tails to a serving plate. Use the steaming liquid as a dipping sauce. Serve warm.

Copycat Old Bay Seasoning

To make your own copycat Old Bay Seasoning, combine 1 tablespoon celery salt, 2 tablespoons smoked paprika, 1½ teaspoons mustard powder, ¾ teaspoon cayenne pepper, 1 teaspoon black pepper, ¼ teaspoon ground bay leaves, ⅛ teaspoon ground cinnamon, ⅛ teaspoon ground cloves, and ⅛ teaspoon ground nutmeg. Store in an airtight container.

Baked Crab Cakes

Serves 4

Per Serving

Calories	204
Fat	11g
Sodium	639mg
Carbohydrates	3g
Fiber	0g
Sugar	2g
Protein	20g

Differences in Crabmeat

There are different kinds of crabmeat found at the grocery store. You can find fresh crabmeat in the seafood section, but there are also canned varieties in the canned seafood and fish section. Although backfin and claw are acceptable choices, lump crabmeat consists of large, tender pieces that hold their shape well, creating crab cakes with noticeable chunks and a satisfying bite.

These low-carb crab cakes are so versatile! Enjoy them with homemade Thousand Island Dressing (Chapter 9) or even on a low-carb slider bun. Or if you are feeling a little fancy, make a Benedict version using the crab cake as a bread substitute and then topping with a slice of fresh tomato, a poached egg, and some hollandaise sauce.

12 ounces lump crabmeat

4 ounces cream cheese, room temperature

1 large egg, whisked

⅓ cup crushed pork rinds

1 teaspoon prepared horseradish

¼ teaspoon ground black pepper

1 medium shallot, peeled and diced

1 tablespoon fresh orange juice (about ½ orange)

1. Preheat oven to 350°F. Line a baking sheet with parchment paper.
2. In a medium bowl, combine all ingredients. Using a 2-tablespoon cookie scooper, scoop twelve portions of crabmeat mixture onto parchment paper. Lightly press down on each portion. Spray tops of crab cakes with nonstick butter cooking spray.
3. Bake 25 minutes, then broil on high 3 minutes. Let rest 3 minutes and serve warm.

CHAPTER 7

Vegetarian Mains and Sides

Loaded Mashed Cauliflower 152
Lower-Carb Garlic Mashed Potatoes 153
Air Fryer Avocado Fries 154
Cast Iron Brussels Sprouts 155
Veggie Sammie 156
Roasted Halloumi and Cauliflower 158
Oven-Roasted Parmesan Broccoli 159
Dilled Roasted Carrots 160
Roasted Radishes 161
Summer Squash Casserole 162
Sweet and Tangy Braised Red Cabbage 163
Zucchini Tacos 165
Baked Onion Rings 166
Bean Burger Patties 167
Tex-Mex Zucchini Boats 168
Protein Lentil Bowls 169
Blistered Tomatoes 170
Grilled Green Tomatoes 171
Portobello Pizzas 172
Quick-Pickled Red Onions 174
Slow Cooker Mushrooms 174

Loaded Mashed Cauliflower

Serves 4	
Per Serving	
Calories	161
Fat	9g
Sodium	471mg
Carbohydrates	11g
Fiber	4g
Sugar	4g
Protein	8g

This creamy, low-carb alternative to traditional mashed potatoes is blended with simple seasonings. The flavored cream cheese adds to the depth of flavor and gives the cauliflower some thickness. Topped with Cheddar cheese and green onions, it's a comforting side dish that only feels indulgent.

1 large head cauliflower, cut into florets (approximately 4 cups)

1 tablespoon unsalted butter

½ teaspoon salt

¼ teaspoon ground black pepper

2 tablespoons onion and chive cream cheese

½ cup shredded Cheddar cheese

¼ cup sliced green onion (green parts only)

1. Steam cauliflower 10 minutes or until tender.
2. Add to a food processor with butter, salt, black pepper, and cream cheese. Pulse until smooth. Add Cheddar cheese. Pulse until combined.
3. Transfer ingredients to a serving dish and garnish with green onion greens. Serve warm.

Lower-Carb Garlic Mashed Potatoes

Balancing creamy texture with a reduction in carbs, this side dish blends a russet potato, sweet potato, and cauliflower for a lighter, healthier twist on the classic. This colorful mash delivers subtle sweetness and earthy flavor with a hint of garlic while still checking the box as a comfort food.

Serves 6

Per Serving

Calories	224
Fat	13g
Sodium	456mg
Carbohydrates	23g
Fiber	5g
Sugar	5g
Protein	5g

1 medium head cauliflower, cut into florets (approximately 3 cups)

1 large sweet potato, peeled and cubed

1 large russet potato, scrubbed and diced

4 cloves garlic, peeled

3 tablespoons unsalted butter

½ cup heavy cream

1 teaspoon salt

1 teaspoon ground black pepper

1. In a large pot, add cauliflower, sweet potato, russet potato, and garlic. Fill with water to cover vegetables. Bring to boil. Simmer, covered, until sweet potatoes are fork-tender.
2. Drain pot. Add butter, cream, salt, and black pepper. Using a hand-held masher or ricer, mash until desired consistency.
3. Transfer to 6 bowls and serve warm.

Air Fryer Avocado Fries

Serves 2

Per Serving

Calories	235
Fat	16g
Sodium	264mg
Carbohydrates	13g
Fiber	7g
Sugar	1g
Protein	9g

What Is Chickpea Flour?

Chickpea flour is made from ground dried chickpeas. It is naturally gluten-free and high in protein, making it a nutritious alternative to wheat flour. Although lower in carbs than the wheat variety, it is still not without carbs. It is good used in moderation as a substitute for traditional flour.

Crispy on the outside and creamy on the inside, these "fries" are made with avocado slices coated in a flavorful blend of chickpea flour, cumin, and salt. Air fried with a touch of avocado oil, they're a low-carb, nutrient-rich appetizer or snack.

2 teaspoons avocado oil, divided

1 large egg

¼ cup chickpea flour

¼ cup nutritional yeast

¼ teaspoon salt

¼ teaspoon ground cumin

1 large avocado, peeled, pitted, and cut into 8 sections

1. Preheat an air fryer to 375°F for 3 minutes. Grease the air fryer basket with 1 teaspoon oil.
2. Whisk egg in a small dish. In a medium dish, add flour, nutritional yeast, salt, and cumin.
3. Dip 4 avocado sections in egg, then coat with flour mixture. Place in air fryer basket and air fry 5 minutes.
4. Transfer to a serving plate and repeat with remaining avocado sections, greasing air fryer basket with remaining oil before air frying. Serve warm.

Cast Iron Brussels Sprouts

You might actually get your family to try Brussels sprouts with this recipe. Quartering the sprouts helps coat them with the fresh orange juice for a bright, savory-sweet finish. Cooked until crispy in a hot cast iron skillet, this dish delivers bold flavor with minimal ingredients and maximum flavor.

Serves 6

Per Serving

Calories	61
Fat	2g
Sodium	214mg
Carbohydrates	9g
Fiber	3g
Sugar	3g
Protein	3g

1 tablespoon avocado oil

1½ pounds (about 24) Brussels sprouts, quartered

Juice and zest of 1 large navel orange

½ teaspoon smoked paprika

½ teaspoon salt

¼ teaspoon ground black pepper

1. Preheat oven to 375°F.
2. Heat oil in a large oven safe skillet over medium-high heat. Add Brussels sprouts to skillet. Toss in juice, zest, paprika, salt, and black pepper. Toss and allow to brown 5 minutes.
3. Move skillet to oven and roast 20 minutes. Serve warm.

Cast Iron Skillets

There is a reason that cast iron skillets have been passed down for generations. They are a timeless kitchen essential that stands the test of time. They are versatile (they can be used for searing, baking, frying, and roasting) and naturally nonstick when seasoned properly. These skillets distribute heat evenly and can be used both on the stovetop and in the oven. Heck, you can even take one to your campfire!

Veggie Sammie

Serves 4

Per Serving

Calories	358
Fat	17g
Sodium	1,265mg
Carbohydrates	50g
Fiber	32g
Sugar	4g
Protein	21g

This sandwich layers a flavorful black bean spread—blended with lime juice, cumin, and garlic—onto toasted low-carb bread and then stacks on roasted red peppers, cucumber slices, feta cheese, and crisp broccoli sprouts. Add a swipe of creamy mayonnaise and this vibrant, protein-packed sandwich is both satisfying and craveable.

1 (15-ounce) can black beans, drained and rinsed

Juice from ½ medium lime

½ teaspoon ground cumin

2 cloves garlic, peeled and minced

¼ teaspoon salt

¼ teaspoon ground black pepper

8 slices seeded low-carb bread, toasted

4 tablespoons mayonnaise

8 slices roasted red pepper

4 tablespoons crumbled feta cheese

1 small cucumber, cut into 16 slices

1 cup broccoli sprouts

1. In a food processor, add beans, lime juice, cumin, garlic, salt, and black pepper. Pulse until smooth.
2. For each sandwich, spread a slice of bread with black bean mixture. Spread another slice with 1 tablespoon mayonnaise. Build each sandwich on bread slice with black bean mixture with 2 roasted red pepper slices, 1 tablespoon feta cheese, 4 cucumber slices, and ¼ cup broccoli sprouts. Top with slice of bread with mayonnaise.
3. Slice each sandwich in half and serve.

Roasted Halloumi and Cauliflower

Serves 6

Per Serving

Calories	184
Fat	13g
Sodium	552mg
Carbohydrates	7g
Fiber	2g
Sugar	4g
Protein	10g

What Is Halloumi?

Halloumi is a salty and savory semi-firm brined cheese. Made from a mix of sheep's and goat's milks, it has a high melting point, so you can grill or pan-fry it without it melting down and losing its shape. This cheese, popular in a lot of Middle Eastern dishes, can be found at most grocers in the specialty cheese section.

This vibrant, savory dish featuring golden cauliflower florets and crispy-edged Halloumi cheese is tossed in a freshly squeezed orange juice and avocado oil marinade. With a touch of salt and black pepper, it's a simple yet flavorful side or light main course.

2 tablespoons avocado oil

Juice of 1 large navel orange

½ teaspoon salt

¼ teaspoon ground black pepper

1 medium head cauliflower, cut into small florets

8 ounces Halloumi cheese, cut into 12 slices

1. Preheat oven to 375°F. Line a baking sheet with parchment paper.
2. In a medium bowl, combine oil, orange juice, salt, and black pepper. Toss in cauliflower florets. Refrigerate florets in marinade 30 minutes.
3. Remove cauliflower florets from marinade and scatter over baking sheet. Bake 30 minutes.
4. Top cauliflower with cheese and place under broiler on low 5 minutes. Let rest 5 minutes and serve warm.

Oven-Roasted Parmesan Broccoli

These roasted florets are tossed with avocado oil, lemon juice, and a generous sprinkling of Parmesan cheese, then roasted until golden and slightly crispy. Naturally low in carbs and high in fiber, this simple, savory side dish turns everyday broccoli into a crowd-pleasing favorite.

Serves 4

Per Serving

Calories	130
Fat	8g
Sodium	698mg
Carbohydrates	11g
Fiber	4g
Sugar	3g
Protein	5g

2 tablespoons avocado oil

Juice of 1 medium lemon

1 teaspoon salt

¼ teaspoon ground black pepper

3 tablespoons grated vegetarian Parmesan cheese, divided

1 large head broccoli, cut into 1-inch florets

1. Preheat oven to 450°F. Line a baking sheet with parchment paper.
2. In a large bowl, whisk together oil, lemon juice, salt, black pepper, and 1½ tablespoons Parmesan cheese. Add broccoli florets and toss.
3. Scatter on baking sheet and bake 20 minutes.
4. Remove from oven and garnish with remaining Parmesan cheese. Serve warm.

Dilled Roasted Carrots

Serves 4

Per Serving

Calories	112
Fat	5g
Sodium	547mg
Carbohydrates	16g
Fiber	5g
Sugar	8g
Protein	2g

Carrot Greens Uses

If your carrots came with those beautiful green toppers, don't throw them away, as they are completely edible and packed with vitamin A, vitamin C, dietary fiber, calcium, and iron. You can add them as a garnish to this dish or save them for your next salad or simple pesto or even your next protein smoothie!

These carrots are perfectly roasted until tender, which helps bring out their natural sweetness. The herbaceous flavor of the dill enhances that sweetness, creating a simple yet flavorful side dish.

1 bunch large carrots (8–10), scrubbed and greens removed

2 tablespoons avocado oil

1 teaspoon salt

¼ teaspoon ground black pepper

1 tablespoon chopped fresh dill

1. Preheat oven to 450°F. Line a baking sheet with parchment paper.
2. Slice carrots in half lengthwise. Add to a large bowl, toss in oil, and season with salt and black pepper. Place on baking sheet and bake 25 minutes.
3. Remove from oven and garnish with dill. Serve warm.

Roasted Radishes

This low-carb alternative to roasted potatoes will be a shock when you try them for the first time. When roasted, radishes lose their peppery taste and their flavor turns slightly sweet and buttery.

Serves 6

Per Serving

Calories	43
Fat	3g
Sodium	320mg
Carbohydrates	3g
Fiber	1g
Sugar	1g
Protein	1g

1½ pounds radishes, trimmed and halved

2 tablespoons avocado oil

1 teaspoon salt

½ teaspoon ground black pepper

1 tablespoon Italian seasoning

1. Preheat oven to 425°F. Line a baking sheet with parchment paper.
2. In a medium bowl, toss radish halves in oil. Season with salt, black pepper, and Italian seasoning. Transfer to baking sheet.
3. Bake 25 minutes. Flip radishes and bake an additional 25 minutes. Serve warm.

Summer Squash Casserole

Serves 8

Per Serving

Calories	164
Fat	11g
Sodium	364mg
Carbohydrates	10g
Fiber	5g
Sugar	4g
Protein	10g

If you have found yourself with a bumper crop of yellow squash from your summer garden and are tired of steaming them, try them in this take on a traditional Southern casserole. Using low-carb bread will fool the best of them!

3 medium yellow summer squash, sliced into half-moons

2 tablespoons water

4 slices low-carb white bread, cubed

1 cup whole milk

3 tablespoons unsalted butter, melted

2 large eggs, whisked

½ teaspoon salt

½ teaspoon ground black pepper

1 small yellow onion, peeled and grated

1 cup shredded sharp Cheddar cheese

1. Preheat oven to 350°F. Spray an 8" × 8" baking dish with nonstick cooking spray.
2. Add squash and water to a medium microwave-safe bowl. Microwave on high 4 minutes. Drain completely.
3. In a large bowl, soak bread cubes in milk and melted butter until saturated. Add eggs, salt, black pepper, onion, cheese, and squash. Pour into baking dish.
4. Bake 30 minutes. Let rest 15 minutes to set. Serve warm.

Sweet and Tangy Braised Red Cabbage

This low-carb, high-fiber dish pairs perfectly with sausages and is a colorful addition to any plate. It has the right balance of natural sweetness from the cabbage and a tangy kick from the vinegar.

Serves 6

Per Serving

Calories	76
Fat	2g
Sodium	427mg
Carbohydrates	20g
Fiber	3g
Sugar	6g
Protein	2g

1 tablespoon avocado oil

1 medium red onion, peeled and thinly sliced

1 medium head red cabbage, cored and chopped

1 teaspoon salt

½ teaspoon ground black pepper

½ teaspoon ground cumin

½ cup apple cider vinegar

¼ cup Swerve brown sugar

1. In a large saucepan, heat oil over medium-high heat. Add red onion and sauté 3 minutes or until tender. Add red cabbage, salt, black pepper, and cumin. Sauté 20 minutes, stirring occasionally.
2. Stir in vinegar and sugar. Sauté 15 minutes. Serve warm.

Zucchini Tacos

These tacos feature a flavorful medley of sautéed zucchini, onions, and spices, all nestled inside crispy cheese taco shells made by baking shredded cheese until golden and crispy. They are a deliciously low-carb and vegetarian twist on taco night.

Serves 6

Per Serving

Calories	320
Fat	22g
Sodium	749mg
Carbohydrates	10g
Fiber	4g
Sugar	6g
Protein	15g

3 cups shredded Mexican-style cheese

1 medium zucchini, diced

1 small yellow onion, peeled and sliced

2 tablespoons avocado oil

1 teaspoon cumin

½ teaspoon salt

¼ teaspoon ground black pepper

½ cup rinsed black beans, warmed

1 cup shredded lettuce

1 cup salsa

½ cup sour cream

1. Preheat oven to 425°F. Line a large baking sheet with parchment paper.
2. Arrange six circles, each consisting of ½ cup cheese, on baking sheet. Bake 17 minutes. Remove from oven and let cool 1–2 minutes until cool enough to handle. Drape each circle over a wooden spoon handle to form shape of a classic hard taco shell. Let cool and harden.
3. Reduce oven temperature to 375°F. Line a baking sheet with parchment paper.
4. In a medium bowl, toss zucchini, onion, oil, cumin, salt, and black pepper. Arrange on baking sheet. Bake 20 minutes. Let cool 5 minutes.
5. Build tacos by spooning zucchini mixture into cheese shells. Top with black beans, lettuce, salsa, and sour cream. Serve immediately.

Baked Onion Rings

Serves 4

Per Serving

Calories	188
Fat	13g
Sodium	428mg
Carbohydrates	8g
Fiber	2g
Sugar	2g
Protein	9g

This low-carb, oven-crisped version of classic deep-fried onion rings pairs perfectly with the Veggie Sammie (see recipe in this chapter) and the Bunless Beef Sliders (Chapter 5). And don't forget to serve them with your favorite no-sugar-added dipping sauce.

1 cup almond flour

1 cup grated vegetarian Parmesan cheese

1 tablespoon baking powder

2 large eggs, whisked

2 tablespoons heavy cream

1 large sweet onion, peeled and sliced into rings

1. Preheat oven to 400°F. Line a baking sheet with parchment paper.
2. In a medium bowl, combine flour, Parmesan cheese, and baking powder. In another medium bowl, combine eggs and cream.
3. Dip onion rings in wet mixture. Dredge onion rings in dry mixture. Place on baking sheet.
4. Spray onions with nonstick cooking spray. Bake 10 minutes. Flip onions. Spray again with nonstick cooking spray. Bake an additional 10 minutes. Serve warm.

Bean Burger Patties

These patties are a hearty plant-based option packed with protein and fiber, combining tempeh and black beans for a satisfying texture. Seasoned with mustard, onion, and vegan cheese, these patties deliver bold flavor without excess carbs. Perfect for a nutritious, low-carb vegan meal or burger alternative.

Serves 4

Per Serving

Calories	365
Fat	15g
Sodium	952mg
Carbohydrates	20g
Fiber	5g
Sugar	1g
Protein	15g

1 flax egg
1 (8-ounce) package tempeh
1 cup smashed canned black beans
1 teaspoon salt
½ teaspoon ground black pepper
½ teaspoon ground mustard
¼ cup grated yellow onion
½ cup grated vegan cheese
2 tablespoons avocado oil

1. Preheat oven to 350°F.
2. In a medium bowl, combine all ingredients except oil. Form mixture into four balls.
3. In a large ovenproof skillet, heat oil over medium-high heat. Add balls and press down until ¼-inch-thick patties form. Cook 3 minutes. Flip and cook an additional 3 minutes. Transfer patties to the oven and bake 10 minutes.
4. Remove from oven and serve warm.

What Is a Flax Egg?

A flax egg is a plant-based egg substitute made by mixing 1 tablespoon ground flaxseed with 3 tablespoons water and letting this sit about 10 minutes until it becomes gel-like. It is a 1:1 substitution for one large chicken egg.

Tex-Mex Zucchini Boats

Serves 8

Per Serving

Calories	211
Fat	11g
Sodium	495mg
Carbohydrates	16g
Fiber	5g
Sugar	5g
Protein	11g

These colorful, vegetable-packed zucchini boats are filled with a zesty mix of black beans, corn, bell pepper, tomatoes, cumin, and cilantro. Topped with melted cheese, they're a flavorful, wholesome take on classic Tex-Mex flavors.

4 medium zucchini, halved lengthwise

2 tablespoons avocado oil

1 medium yellow bell pepper, seeded and diced

1 large shallot, peeled and minced

1 cup canned corn, drained

1 cup canned black beans, rinsed

1 (14.5-ounce) can petite diced tomatoes, drained

1 teaspoon cumin

½ teaspoon salt

¼ cup chopped fresh cilantro

2 cups shredded Mexican cheese blend

1. Preheat oven to 400°F.
2. Using a spoon, hollow out the middle of each zucchini half, creating a boat. Place boats in an ungreased 9" × 13" baking dish.
3. In a large skillet over medium-high heat, add oil. Add bell pepper and shallot and stir-fry 3 minutes. Add corn, beans, tomatoes, cumin, salt, and cilantro and cook an additional 3 minutes.
4. Spoon mixture into zucchini boats. Cover with aluminum foil. Bake 20 minutes. Remove foil. Top boats with cheese and bake an additional 10 minutes. Serve warm.

Protein Lentil Bowls

This hearty, nutrient-packed meal balances plant-based protein with vibrant vegetables and bold flavor. High in protein and fiber, this bowl is a satisfying, low-carb-friendly option for lunch or dinner. Prep these bowls for the week and then cook your eggs when ready to serve.

Serves 4

Per Serving

Calories	678
Fat	53g
Sodium	1,156mg
Carbohydrates	25g
Fiber	9g
Sugar	4g
Protein	22g

4 cups fresh spring mix greens

1 cup Kickin' Dijon Mustard Dressing (Chapter 9)

2 medium Roma tomatoes, diced

½ teaspoon salt

½ teaspoon ground black pepper

2 cups cooked green lentils

1 cup jarred pickled giardiniera

4 ounces goat cheese, crumbled

4 large eggs, cooked over medium

1. In a large bowl, toss greens with dressing. Distribute among individual serving bowls.
2. Season tomatoes with salt and black pepper.
3. Imagine each bowl is a pie and distribute lentils, giardiniera, tomatoes, and goat cheese in their own pie section. Top with a cooked egg. Serve.

Blistered Tomatoes

Serves 4

Per Serving

Calories	51
Fat	4g
Sodium	296mg
Carbohydrates	5g
Fiber	1g
Sugar	3g
Protein	1g

Blistered Tomatoes are cooked quickly in a hot pan until they burst, releasing their juicy sweetness and charred flavor, and then enhanced with a drizzle of olive oil and fresh herbs. This vibrant dish makes a perfect topping for baked fish or roasted chicken, or it can be a flavorful addition to salads.

1 (16-ounce) pack Campari tomatoes, halved

1 tablespoon avocado oil

½ teaspoon salt

¼ teaspoon ground black pepper

1. Preheat oven to 400°F. Line a baking sheet with parchment paper.
2. In a medium bowl, toss halved tomatoes with oil, salt, and black pepper. Place on baking sheet.
3. Bake 15 minutes. Serve warm.

Grilled Green Tomatoes

There is something about grilling vegetables and fruits that brings out their natural flavors, added with a little smokiness. These tomatoes are delicious as a side dish, or they can be enjoyed on a burger, in a caprese salad, or diced and placed in Fish Tacos (Chapter 6).

Serves 4	
Per Serving	
Calories	49
Fat	3g
Sodium	16mg
Carbohydrates	74g
Fiber	1g
Sugar	5g
Protein	1g

½ cup avocado oil

¼ cup apple cider vinegar

2 teaspoons pure maple syrup

1 teaspoon coconut aminos

½ teaspoon salt

1 pound green tomatoes, sliced into ¼-inch rounds

1. In a large bowl, combine oil, vinegar, syrup, coconut aminos, and salt. Add tomato slices to marinade and refrigerate 30 minutes.
2. Heat a grilling pan over medium-high heat. Remove tomato rounds from marinade and add to grill. Grill 2 minutes on each side or until tender. Serve warm.

Dressing Up Green Tomatoes

If your grilled tomatoes need a little dressing up, finish them with some goat cheese crumbles once they come off the grill. Or sprinkle on a little grated Parmesan cheese and garnish with some fresh basil.

Portobello Pizzas

Serves 2

Per Serving

Calories	320
Fat	22g
Sodium	879mg
Carbohydrates	13g
Fiber	3g
Sugar	6g
Protein	14g

Parchment Paper Substitute

If parchment paper feels wasteful to you, an alternative is available. Silicone nonstick baking mats are reusable, cleanup is easy, and most are dishwasher-safe.

These portobello mushroom pizzas use large mushroom caps as the crust for a low-carb, gluten-free alternative to traditional pizza night. Baked until bubbly, they are a quick and savory option for a weeknight dinner.

2 large portobello mushroom caps, gills scraped and discarded

1 tablespoon avocado oil

2 tablespoons grated vegetarian Parmesan cheese

⅓ cup no-sugar-added marinara sauce

1 medium green bell pepper, seeded and diced

1 (2.5-ounce) can sliced black olives, drained

1 cup shredded mozzarella cheese

1. Preheat oven to 375°F. Line a baking sheet with parchment paper.
2. Add mushroom caps to baking sheet. Brush insides and rim of each cap with oil. Sprinkle with Parmesan cheese.
3. Spread marinara over mushroom caps. Distribute bell pepper and black olives among caps. Top each with ½ cup mozzarella cheese.
4. Bake 15 minutes or until cheese is melted. Transfer to plates and serve warm.

Quick-Pickled Red Onions

Yields 1 cup

Per Serving (Serving size: 1/4 cup)

Calories	16
Fat	0g
Sodium	59mg
Carbohydrates	4g
Fiber	1g
Sugar	2g
Protein	0g

Delicious on bunless burgers, morning eggs, salads, and even tacos, this tangy condiment is simply irresistible!

- 1 large red onion, peeled and thinly sliced
- 1/4 cup water
- 1/4 cup apple cider vinegar
- 1 tablespoon honey
- 2 teaspoons black peppercorns
- 1 teaspoon salt
- 1/4 teaspoon red pepper flakes

1. Place onions in a glass jar.
2. In a small saucepan over high heat, add remaining ingredients. Bring to a boil. Reduce heat to low and simmer 1 minute. Pour into jar over onions. Let cool 30 minutes.
3. Transfer to a lidded container and refrigerate up to 1 week.

Slow Cooker Mushrooms

Serves 6

Per Serving

Calories	100
Fat	6g
Sodium	708mg
Carbohydrates	7g
Fiber	2g
Sugar	4g
Protein	5g

If you are planning to throw a few steaks on the grill for dinner, make sure you start these mushrooms early. If you want variety, use half white mushrooms and half baby bellas. These are a perfect side to an outdoor meal accompanied by a lightly tossed salad.

- 2 pounds whole medium white mushrooms
- 2 cups vegetable broth
- 1/2 cup dry red wine
- 1/4 cup apple cider vinegar
- 3 tablespoons salted butter
- 4 cloves garlic, peeled and minced
- 1 teaspoon salt
- 1/4 teaspoon crushed red pepper flakes
- 1 tablespoon Italian seasoning

Place all ingredients in a 6-quart slow cooker. Cover and cook on low 6 hours. Serve warm.

CHAPTER 8

Soups, Stews, and Chilis

Homemade Chicken Broth 176
Homemade Beef Broth 177
Bacon Cauli Fauxtato Soup 178
Chorizo and Black Bean Soup 179
Creamy Broccoli Soup 181
Wild Mushroom Soup 182
Fire-Roasted Tomato Soup 183
Thai Coconut Chicken Soup 184
Cheeseburger Soup 185
Southern Potlikker Soup 186
Navy Bean Soup 187
Easy French Onion Soup 188
Duck and Butternut Squash Stew 190
Vegetable Soup 191
Carrot and Ginger Miso Soup 192
Quick Miso Soup 193
Tex-Mex Turkey Chili 194
Fish Stew 195
Crab Bisque 197
Manhattan Clam Chowder 198
Cowgirl Cactus Chili 199
Chicken Chili Verde 200
Beef Stew 201

Homemade Chicken Broth

Yields 4 cups

Per Serving (Serving size: 1 cup)

Calories	19
Fat	1g
Sodium	593mg
Carbohydrates	1g
Fiber	0g
Sugar	0g
Protein	2g

This broth is a rich, comforting base made by simmering chicken bones with vegetables, herbs, and spices several hours to extract deep flavor and nutrients. It is great for prep day. Cook a whole chicken, then remove the meat for meals and salads and boil the bones to use to make a soup.

Bones from a whole chicken, meat removed

2 large carrots, cut into 1-inch chunks

2 stalks celery, including stems, cut into 1-inch sections

1 large yellow onion, peeled and cut into 6 wedges

2 bay leaves

1 teaspoon dried thyme

1 teaspoon salt

5 cups water

1. Add all ingredients to a large heavy-bottomed pot. Bring to a boil. Reduce heat to low and simmer, uncovered, 4 hours.
2. Strain and discard vegetables and solids.
3. Refrigerate broth, covered, overnight. The next day, skim fat layer from the top of broth and discard. Refrigerate broth up to 4 days or freeze up to 6 months.

Homemade Beef Broth

If you can't find beef soup bones on display in your grocery store, ask your local butcher. Many specialty grocery stores also carry them. If you can't find them, oxtail or neck bones are a good substitute.

Yields 4 cups

Per Serving (Serving size: 1 cup)

Calories	19
Fat	1g
Sodium	589mg
Carbohydrates	1g
Fiber	0g
Sugar	0g
Protein	1g

3 pounds beef soup bones

2 large carrots, cut into 1-inch chunks

2 stalks celery, including stems, cut into 1-inch sections

1 large yellow onion, peeled and cut into 6 wedges

2 bay leaves

1 teaspoon apple cider vinegar

1 teaspoon salt

5 cups water

1. Add all ingredients to a large heavy-bottomed pot. Bring to a boil. Reduce heat to low and simmer, uncovered, 4 hours.
2. Strain and discard vegetables and solids.
3. Refrigerate broth, covered, overnight. The next day, skim fat layer from the top of broth and discard. Refrigerate broth up to 4 days or freeze up to 6 months.

Bacon Cauli Fauxtato Soup

Serves 4

Per Serving

Calories	411
Fat	35g
Sodium	1,885mg
Carbohydrates	10g
Fiber	2g
Sugar	5g
Protein	11g

You will never miss the potato in this low-carb version of classic potato soup. The cauliflower contributes to the creaminess and the bacon adds that salty touch. Read the ingredient label on your bacon choice, as some are full of sugars.

3 tablespoons unsalted butter
1 small head cauliflower, chopped
1 small yellow onion, peeled and diced
3 stalks celery, chopped
3 cloves garlic, peeled and minced
6 slices no-sugar-added bacon, divided
4 cups chicken broth
1 teaspoon salt
1 teaspoon ground black pepper
1 tablespoon fresh thyme leaves
1 cup heavy whipping cream
1 tablespoon cooking sherry

1. In a large pot, heat butter over medium heat. Add cauliflower, onion, celery, garlic, and 1 slice bacon. Cook 4 minutes, stirring.
2. Add broth, salt, black pepper, and thyme. Bring to a boil. Reduce heat to low and let simmer 30 minutes or until cauliflower is tender.
3. Using an immersion blender, blend until smooth. Add cream and sherry. Stir. Let simmer 15 minutes.
4. In a medium skillet, cook remaining bacon until crispy and then crumble it.
5. Ladle soup into bowls and garnish with crisp bacon. Serve warm.

Chorizo and Black Bean Soup

The great thing about ground chorizo is that it is pre-seasoned with deliciously warm spices so you don't have to add much flavor up front. Thanks to the chorizo and black beans, this soup is high in protein and fiber—making it hearty and satisfying. While not ultra-low in carbs due to the beans, it's still a balanced option for those looking to prioritize protein. Enjoy it as is, or top with sour cream and/or grated cotija cheese for a creamy finish.

Serves 4

Per Serving

Calories	711
Fat	48g
Sodium	2,885mg
Carbohydrates	26g
Fiber	8g
Sugar	4g
Protein	36g

2 tablespoons avocado oil
1 pound ground chorizo
1 small yellow onion, peeled and diced
1 small red bell pepper, seeded and diced
½ cup grated carrots
3 cloves garlic, peeled and minced
4 cups chicken broth
½ teaspoon salt
½ teaspoon ground black pepper
¼ cup chopped fresh cilantro
1 (15-ounce) can black beans, drained and rinsed
1 tablespoon cooking sherry

1. In a large pot, heat oil over medium heat. Add chorizo, onion, bell pepper, carrots, and garlic. Cook 4 minutes, stirring until chorizo is cooked through.
2. Add broth, salt, black pepper, cilantro, and black beans. Bring to a boil. Reduce heat to low and let simmer 40 minutes. Stir in sherry.
3. Ladle into individual serving bowls and serve warm.

Don't Like Cilantro?

Some people possess a gene that makes them supersensitive to the aldehyde component found in cilantro. They describe cilantro as "soapy tasting." No worries, you can substitute the cilantro with fresh parsley in this recipe and enjoy it just as well!

Creamy Broccoli Soup

This soup is a velvety mix of tender broccoli, onions, celery, and carrot simmered in a creamy broth and then blended to perfection. This comforting bowl is both nourishing and rich, with the natural flavors of broccoli shining through in every spoonful.

Serves 4

Per Serving

Calories	486
Fat	37g
Sodium	1,812mg
Carbohydrates	19g
Fiber	5g
Sugar	8g
Protein	15g

3 tablespoons unsalted butter

1 medium yellow onion, peeled and diced

2 stalks celery, diced

1 large carrot, peeled and diced

1 small head broccoli

4 cups chicken broth

1 teaspoon salt

½ teaspoon ground black pepper

1 teaspoon dried thyme

1 cup heavy cream

1 tablespoon cooking sherry

1 cup shredded mild Cheddar cheese

1. In a large pot, heat butter over medium heat 1 minute or until melted. Add onion, celery, and carrot. Sauté 3 minutes or until onion is tender.
2. Add broccoli, broth, salt, black pepper, and thyme. Bring to a boil. Reduce heat to medium-low, cover, and simmer 45 minutes. Using an immersion blender (or a stand blender in batches), blend until desired consistency, either completely smooth or a little chunky.
3. Stir in cream and sherry. Simmer an additional 15 minutes.
4. Ladle into individual serving bowls, garnish with cheese, and serve warm.

Don't Skip the Cooking Sherry!

If you ever cook a cream-based soup, add a touch of cooking sherry. Remember that a little goes a long way, but it packs a punch. Cooking sherry adds depth of flavor and a subtle acidity, helping to balance the richness of the cream and enhance the overall taste. Its mild alcohol content evaporates during cooking, leaving behind a savory, slightly sweet complexity.

Wild Mushroom Soup

Serves 4

Per Serving

Calories	336
Fat	29g
Sodium	1,581mg
Carbohydrates	11g
Fiber	2g
Sugar	6g
Protein	5g

Wild Mushroom Soup is a comfort food for many people, with its warming flavors and creamy texture. Pair with a grilled cheese sandwich on low-carb bread for a full meal.

3 tablespoons unsalted butter

1 medium yellow onion, peeled and diced

2 stalks celery, diced

½ cup grated carrots

2 cups sliced baby bella mushrooms

1 cup sliced shiitake mushrooms

1 cup sliced button mushrooms

4 cups chicken broth

1 teaspoon salt

½ teaspoon ground black pepper

2 teaspoons fresh thyme leaves

1 cup heavy cream

1 tablespoon cooking sherry

1. In a large pot, heat butter over medium heat 1 minute or until melted. Add onion, celery, carrots, and mushrooms. Sauté 3 minutes or until onions are tender.
2. Add broth, salt, black pepper, and thyme. Bring to a boil. Reduce heat to low and let simmer 40 minutes. Using an immersion blender (or a stand blender in batches), blend until desired consistency, either completely smooth or a little chunky.
3. Stir in cream and sherry. Simmer an additional 15 minutes.
4. Ladle into individual serving bowls and serve warm.

Fire-Roasted Tomato Soup

This comforting soup is high in healthy fats and protein-friendly when garnished with grated cheese. And don't forget to add some homemade low-carb croutons!

Serves 4

Per Serving

Calories	341
Fat	28g
Sodium	1,244mg
Carbohydrates	16g
Fiber	4g
Sugar	9g
Protein	4g

2 tablespoons avocado oil

1 medium yellow onion, peeled and diced

1 medium red bell pepper, seeded and diced

1 teaspoon salt

¼ teaspoon ground black pepper

1 tablespoon Italian seasoning

2 (14.5-ounce) cans fire-roasted tomatoes, including juice

1 cup chicken broth

1 cup heavy cream

1 teaspoon cooking sherry

1. In a large pot, heat oil over medium heat. Add onion and bell pepper. Sauté 3 minutes or until onion is tender.
2. Add salt, black pepper, Italian seasoning, tomatoes and juice, and broth. Bring to a boil. Reduce heat to low and let simmer, covered, 45 minutes. Using an immersion blender (or a stand blender in batches), blend until smooth.
3. Stir in cream and sherry. Simmer an additional 15 minutes.
4. Ladle into individual serving bowls and serve warm.

Homemade Croutons

To make your own low-carb croutons: Dice 4 slices low-carb bread. Toss in 2 tablespoons melted butter, ⅛ teaspoon salt, and 1 teaspoon Italian seasoning. Spread bread dices on a baking sheet and bake 6 minutes at 375°F. Toss bread and bake an additional 6 minutes.

Thai Coconut Chicken Soup

Serves 4

Per Serving

Calories	474
Fat	34g
Sodium	2,393mg
Carbohydrates	13g
Fiber	2g
Sugar	4g
Protein	27g

Chili Threads

Also known as shilgochu, chili threads are thin, delicate strips of dried chili pepper. If you want to add a little flair and some extra heat to your soup presentation, use these as a garnish.

Also known as tom kha gai, this tangy-sweet soup warms you from the inside out. Well-balanced and full of protein and nutrient-rich ingredients, this recipe features a creamy, aromatic blend of coconut milk, lemongrass, ginger, and tender chicken. And if you like heat, add those jalapeño seeds to your soup.

2 tablespoons coconut oil
2 green onions, sliced (white and green parts separated)
1 large carrot, diced
3 cups sliced shiitake mushrooms
1 medium jalapeño, seeded and thinly sliced
1 (1-inch) piece ginger, peeled and thinly sliced
2 teaspoons lemongrass paste
2 cloves garlic, peeled and minced
4 cups chicken broth
1 (13.5-ounce) can full-fat coconut milk
1 teaspoon salt
2 tablespoons fish sauce
½ cup chopped fresh cilantro
1 pound chicken thighs, cut into 1-inch cubes
1 medium lime, quartered

1. In a large pot, heat oil over medium-high heat. Add green onion whites, carrot, mushrooms, and jalapeño. Sauté 3 minutes or until green onion whites are tender.
2. Add remaining ingredients (except green onion greens and lime) to pot and bring to a boil. Reduce heat to low and let simmer 45 minutes.
3. Ladle into individual serving bowls. Garnish each bowl with green onion greens and a squeeze of lime quarter. Serve warm.

Cheeseburger Soup

This hearty and comforting soup is made with all things drive-through—without the buns! It captures the flavors of a classic cheeseburger in soup form, making it a perfect cozy meal for chilly days.

Serves 4

Per Serving

Calories	411
Fat	24g
Sodium	1,878mg
Carbohydrates	10g
Fiber	3g
Sugar	5g
Protein	32g

1 tablespoon avocado oil

1 medium yellow onion, peeled and diced

1 medium green bell pepper, seeded and diced

1 pound 80/20 ground beef

2 cups halved cherry tomatoes

1 teaspoon ground mustard

1 teaspoon garlic powder

1 teaspoon salt

1 teaspoon ground black pepper

4 cups beef broth

2 cups shredded iceberg lettuce

½ cup diced dill pickles

1 cup shredded mild Cheddar cheese

1. In a large pot, heat oil over medium heat 1 minute. Add onion and bell pepper. Sauté 3 minutes or until onion is tender.
2. Add beef and sauté 3–4 minutes until browned. Drain and discard excess liquid.
3. Add tomatoes, mustard, garlic powder, salt, black pepper, and broth. Bring to a boil. Reduce heat to low and simmer 30 minutes. Add shredded lettuce and simmer, covered, an additional 15 minutes.
4. Ladle into individual serving bowls and garnish with pickles and Cheddar cheese. Serve warm.

Southern Potlikker Soup

Serves 4

Per Serving

Calories	322
Fat	17g
Sodium	3,191mg
Carbohydrates	11g
Fiber	4g
Sugar	4g
Protein	29g

This rustic dish is traditionally made from the liquid left over from cooking collard greens, simmered with smoked meat, beans, and vegetables. This simpler version offers a hearty, savory base with a deep, earthy flavor for a soul-warming soup. Make a batch of gluten-free corn bread to round out the meal.

3 tablespoons unsalted butter

1 medium yellow onion, peeled and diced

2 stalks celery, sliced

1 large carrot, shredded

1 (16-ounce) package ham cubes

4 cloves garlic, peeled and minced

6 cups chopped collard greens, stems removed

1 tablespoon apple cider vinegar

4 cups chicken broth

1 teaspoon salt

1 teaspoon ground black pepper

2 teaspoons hot sauce

1. In a large pot, heat butter over medium heat 1 minute. Add onion, celery, and carrot. Sauté 3 minutes or until onion is tender.
2. Add ham and garlic and sauté 2 minutes. Add remaining ingredients.
3. Bring to a boil. Reduce heat to low and simmer, covered, 45 minutes.
4. Ladle into individual serving bowls and serve warm.

Navy Bean Soup

High in protein and fiber, this soup is a wholesome option, especially when made with minimal added carbs.

Serves 4	
Per Serving	
Calories	521
Fat	21g
Sodium	2,907mg
Carbohydrates	56g
Fiber	14g
Sugar	5g
Protein	28g

3 tablespoons unsalted butter
1 medium yellow onion, peeled and diced
4 cloves garlic, peeled and minced
2 stalks celery, including leaves, sliced
2 large carrots, scrubbed and diced
1 ham hock
4 cups chicken broth
2 (15-ounce) cans navy beans, rinsed, divided
2 bay leaves
1 teaspoon salt
1 teaspoon ground black pepper
1 tablespoon fresh thyme leaves
1 tablespoon cooking sherry

1. In a large pot, heat butter over medium heat 1 minute. Add onion, garlic, celery, and carrots. Sauté 3 minutes or until onion is tender.
2. Add ham hock, broth, 1 can beans, bay leaves, salt, and black pepper. Bring to a boil. Reduce heat to low and simmer, covered, 45 minutes.
3. Remove and discard bay leaves. Remove ham hock and set aside. Using an immersion blender, blend soup until somewhat creamy but still chunky.
4. Add thyme, remaining can beans, sherry, and ham hock. Simmer an additional 30 minutes. Remove ham hock and dice any ham off the bone and add to soup. Discard ham bone.
5. Ladle soup into individual serving bowls and serve warm.

Easy French Onion Soup

Serves 4

Per Serving

Calories	366
Fat	21g
Sodium	1,247mg
Carbohydrates	27g
Fiber	9g
Sugar	9g
Protein	19g

This comforting classic is made with caramelized onions simmered in a rich beef broth, deglazed with white wine, and finished with toasted low-carb bread slices and melted Gruyère cheese. Additional beef broth can be substituted for the wine if you prefer.

3 tablespoons unsalted butter

2 pounds yellow onions, peeled and thinly sliced

½ cup dry white wine (such as chardonnay)

4 cloves garlic, peeled and minced

1 tablespoon fresh thyme leaves, plus more for garnish

4 cups beef broth

1 tablespoon Worcestershire sauce

1 bay leaf

4 slices keto bread, toasted

1 cup grated Gruyère cheese

1. In a large heavy-bottomed pot, heat butter over medium heat 1 minute. Add onions and sauté 25 minutes, stirring often. Deglaze the pot by adding wine and scraping all the bits from the bottom of the pot. Cook, stirring occasionally, an additional 20 minutes.
2. Stir in garlic and thyme. Increase heat to high. Add broth, Worcestershire sauce, and bay leaf and bring to a boil. Reduce heat to medium-low, cover, and simmer 20 minutes.
3. Preheat broiler to high.
4. Ladle soup into individual oven-safe serving bowls, discarding bay leaf. Using a large round cookie cutter, cut out a circle from each slice of bread. Top each bowl of soup with a bread slice and ¼ cup cheese.
5. Place bowls on an ungreased baking sheet and broil 2 minutes or until cheese is melted and browned. Serve warm with a garnish of thyme leaves.

Duck and Butternut Squash Stew

Serves 4

Per Serving

Calories	441
Fat	34g
Sodium	1,606mg
Carbohydrates	13g
Fiber	2g
Sugar	6g
Protein	16g

What Is Fond?

Created through the Maillard reaction (a reaction between sugars and proteins when heated), fond is the flavorful, browned bits that stick to the bottom of a pan after searing meat or vegetables. It's the foundation for many rich sauces and gravies, often deglazed with broth, wine, or water to free up and incorporate those concentrated flavors.

This rich and savory blend of tender cubed duck and sweet butternut squash simmered with aromatic herbs and spices will have your taste buds on fire. Duck breast is a great source of protein and healthy fats, making this stew high in protein and naturally satisfying. While butternut squash contributes some carbohydrates, this dish remains relatively moderate in carbs overall. This stew is perfect for special occasions or chilly nights in.

- 3 tablespoons unsalted butter, divided
- 3 duck breasts (about 2 pounds total), cubed and fat layer trimmed and discarded
- 1 medium white onion, peeled and diced
- 1 stalk celery, sliced
- 1 large carrot, peeled and diced
- 1 medium jalapeño, seeded and sliced
- 1 small butternut squash, peeled, seeded, and diced
- 4 cloves garlic, peeled and minced
- 4 cups chicken broth
- 2 bay leaves
- 1 teaspoon salt
- 1 teaspoon ground black pepper
- 2 teaspoons dried rosemary
- 1 teaspoon dried thyme
- 1 cup heavy cream
- 1 tablespoon cooking sherry

1. In a large pot, heat 1 tablespoon butter over medium heat 1 minute. Add duck cubes and stir-fry 2 minutes or until browned. Transfer to a plate.
2. Add remaining butter, onion, celery, carrot, jalapeño, squash, and garlic. Sauté 3 minutes or until onion is tender, scraping the fond, or bits, from the bottom of the pot. Add broth, bay leaves, salt, black pepper, rosemary, and thyme.
3. Bring to a boil. Reduce heat to low and simmer, covered, 45 minutes. Remove and discard bay leaves. Stir in cream and sherry. Simmer an additional 10 minutes.
4. Ladle into individual serving bowls and serve warm.

Vegetable Soup

In this recipe, the cauliflower replaces the diced potatoes traditionally found in a vegetable soup. This easy-to-make soup is not only chock-full of nutrients but also a one-pot wonder. Tailor this soup to the season or to your taste buds. Green beans, zucchini, and butternut squash are also delicious inclusions.

Serves 4

Per Serving

Calories	186
Fat	8g
Sodium	1,860mg
Carbohydrates	23g
Fiber	5g
Sugar	7g
Protein	7g

2 tablespoons avocado oil

1 medium yellow onion, peeled and diced

1 large carrot, scrubbed and diced

1 cup quartered cauliflower florets

1 (15.25-ounce) can sweet corn kernels, drained

4 cups beef broth

1 (15-ounce) can diced tomatoes, including juice

2 cups fresh baby spinach leaves

2 bay leaves

2 teaspoons Italian seasoning

1 teaspoon salt

½ teaspoon ground black pepper

2 teaspoons Worcestershire sauce

1. In a large pot, heat oil over medium heat 1 minute. Add onion and carrot and sauté 3 minutes or until onion is tender.
2. Add remaining ingredients. Bring to a boil. Reduce heat to low and simmer, covered, 45 minutes. Remove and discard bay leaves.
3. Ladle soup into individual serving bowls and serve warm.

Carrot and Ginger Miso Soup

Serves 4

Per Serving

Calories	363
Fat	31g
Sodium	1,346mg
Carbohydrates	16g
Fiber	5g
Sugar	5g
Protein	6g

Add this soup to your list of favorite comfort foods! The earthy sweetness of carrots blends with the warming spices ginger and cumin and a swirl of heavy cream for richness. It's a nourishing bowl with a bold umami flavor, finished with fresh lime and parsley for a bright lift.

1 tablespoon chili oil
2 tablespoons salted butter
3 large carrots, scrubbed and chopped
1 small yellow onion, peeled and diced
1 (1-inch) piece ginger, peeled and minced
4 cups store-bought miso broth
1 teaspoon salt
1 teaspoon cumin
1⁄8 teaspoon ground cinnamon
1 cup heavy cream
Juice and zest of 1 small lime
1 cup chopped fresh parsley

1. Add chili oil and butter to a large heavy-bottomed pot over medium-high heat. Add carrots, onion, and ginger. Cook 3 minutes or until onion is tender.
2. Add broth, salt, cumin, and cinnamon. Bring to a boil. Reduce heat to low and simmer, covered, 40 minutes. Using an immersion blender, blend pot ingredients until smooth.
3. Stir in cream and lime juice and zest. Simmer an additional 15 minutes.
4. Ladle into individual serving bowls and garnish with parsley. Serve warm.

Quick Miso Soup

This dish is low in calories, high in flavor, and takes under 15 minutes to make. This soup, containing both miso and tofu, seems simple, but is high in nutrients. If you want a little kick, garnish with chili threads or a quick drizzle of chili oil before serving. Most grocers now carry pre-made miso broth. It is usually found in the soup aisle next to the other broths.

Serves 4

Per Serving

Calories	80
Fat	2g
Sodium	660mg
Carbohydrates	10g
Fiber	4g
Sugar	1g
Protein	7g

4 cups store-bought miso broth

¼ cup crumbled nori (dried seaweed)

8 ounces soft tofu, cut into ½-inch cubes

2 green onions, thinly sliced (white and green parts)

1. Add all ingredients to a large heavy-bottomed pot.
2. Bring to a boil. Reduce heat to low and simmer, covered, 5 minutes. Ladle into individual serving bowls and serve warm.

Tex-Mex Turkey Chili

Serves 4

Per Serving

Calories	443
Fat	14g
Sodium	1,251mg
Carbohydrates	45g
Fiber	11g
Sugar	8g
Protein	37g

How Should You Serve Chili?

Although this chili has all the flavors needed for a delicious meal, adding different textures and flavors like sharp shredded cheese, cooling sour cream, and crunchy chopped red onions lends a more satisfying experience.

This chili is a hearty, flavorful dish made with ground turkey, corn, black beans, tomatoes, and a blend of Tex-Mex spices like cumin and chili powder. This is a great recipe to make on a prep day, as chili always tastes better over the next few days after those spices have had time to marry.

1 tablespoon avocado oil
1 medium yellow onion, peeled and diced
1 pound ground turkey
1 pound sliced white mushrooms
2 medium jalapeños, minced
3 cloves garlic, peeled and minced
1 (15-ounce) can black beans, rinsed
1 (14.75-ounce) can creamed corn, including liquid
1 tablespoon chili powder
1 teaspoon salt
1 teaspoon ground cumin
¼ teaspoon cayenne pepper
1 small bunch fresh cilantro, chopped
1 (28-ounce) can chopped tomatoes, including juice

1. In a Dutch oven or large pot, heat oil over medium heat. Add onion and cook 3 minutes or until onion is tender.
2. Add turkey, mushrooms, jalapeños, and garlic. Stir-fry 4–5 minutes until turkey is cooked through.
3. Stir in remaining ingredients. Bring to a boil. Reduce heat to low. Cover and simmer 30 minutes.
4. Stir, ladle into individual serving bowls, and serve warm.

Fish Stew

Though traditional fish stew is often filled with diced potatoes, this delicious version uses lower-carb carrots as a substitute.

Serves 4

Per Serving

Calories	182
Fat	4g
Sodium	1,663mg
Carbohydrates	13g
Fiber	4g
Sugar	7g
Protein	22g

1 tablespoon avocado oil

4 green onions, sliced (both white and green parts)

2 large carrots, scrubbed and diced

1 (14-ounce) can diced tomatoes, including juice

2 tablespoons tomato paste

1 (8-ounce) bottle clam juice

3 cups vegetable broth

1 teaspoon salt

1 teaspoon ground black pepper

1 bay leaf

1 pound skinless cod, cut into 1-inch cubes

1. In a large heavy-bottomed pot, heat oil over medium-high heat 1 minute. Add green onions and carrots. Sauté 3 minutes or until onion whites are tender.
2. Add tomatoes and juice, tomato paste, clam juice, broth, salt, black pepper, and bay leaf. Bring to a boil. Reduce heat to low and simmer, covered, 30 minutes.
3. Add cod. Continue to simmer 5 minutes or until cod easily flakes. Remove bay leaf and discard. Ladle stew into individual serving bowls and serve warm.

Crab Bisque

This luxurious and creamy bisque features tender lump crabmeat simmered with aromatic vegetables, sherry, and a touch of heavy cream for a velvety texture. A hint of seafood seasoning adds depth to each spoonful.

Serves 4

Per Serving

Calories	406
Fat	30g
Sodium	2,732mg
Carbohydrates	13g
Fiber	3g
Sugar	7g
Protein	19g

3 tablespoons unsalted butter

6 green onions, sliced (white and green parts separated)

2 stalks celery, sliced

2 cups chopped cauliflower

1 large carrot, peeled and diced

4 cups vegetable broth

2 tablespoons tomato paste

2 teaspoons fish sauce

1 teaspoon salt

1 teaspoon ground black pepper

¼ teaspoon seafood seasoning

2 teaspoons dried thyme leaves

1 cup heavy cream

2 teaspoons cooking sherry

3 cups cooked lump crabmeat, divided

1. In a large pot, heat butter over medium-high heat 1 minute. Add green onion whites, celery, cauliflower, and carrot. Sauté 3 minutes or until onion whites are tender.
2. Add broth, tomato paste, fish sauce, salt, black pepper, and seafood seasoning. Bring to a boil. Reduce heat to medium-low, cover, and simmer 45 minutes. Using an immersion blender (or a stand blender in batches), blend until pot contents are smooth.
3. Add thyme, cream, sherry, and 2 cups crabmeat. Continue to simmer 10 minutes.
4. Ladle into individual serving bowls and garnish with green onion greens and remaining crabmeat. Serve warm.

Manhattan Clam Chowder

Serves 4

Per Serving

Calories	219
Fat	7g
Sodium	2,517mg
Carbohydrates	25g
Fiber	6g
Sugar	9g
Protein	13g

Manhattan-style clam chowder is a tomato-based soup loaded with vegetables and tender chopped clams for a briny, satisfying spoonful. The tomato base builds a bold, layered flavor that sets it apart from its creamy New England cousin. Naturally lower in carbs and rich in protein, it's a hearty option for any seafood lover.

4 slices no-sugar-added bacon, diced
1 tablespoon unsalted butter
1 medium green bell pepper, seeded and diced
1 small white onion, peeled and diced
2 stalks celery, including leaves, sliced
2 large carrots, scrubbed and diced
4 cloves garlic, peeled and minced
1 teaspoon salt
1 teaspoon ground black pepper
2 teaspoons fresh thyme leaves
1 (28-ounce) can petite diced tomatoes, including juice
2 cups chicken broth
2 (8-ounce) bottles clam juice
1 bay leaf
2 (6.5-ounce) cans chopped clams, including juice

1. In a Dutch oven or large pot, cook bacon 3 minutes over medium-high heat to render fat. Transfer bacon to a paper towel–lined plate.
2. Add butter to bacon fat in pot. Add bell pepper, onion, celery and leaves, carrots, and garlic. Sauté 3 minutes.
3. Add salt, black pepper, thyme, tomatoes and juice, broth, clam juice, and bay leaf.
4. Bring to a boil. Reduce heat to low and simmer 30 minutes. Add clams and juice. Continue to simmer 15 minutes. Remove and discard bay leaf.
5. Ladle soup into individual serving bowls and serve warm.

Cowgirl Cactus Chili

Cayenne pepper and espresso powder play well together to elevate the flavor of this bold, hearty chili. The cactus (nopalitos) adds a touch of natural sweetness that balances the heat. Though the fresh corn does contribute some carbs, this chili is a moderately low-carb option depending on your portion size and dietary needs.

Serves 4

Per Serving

Calories	404
Fat	16g
Sodium	1,265mg
Carbohydrates	35g
Fiber	8g
Sugar	13g
Protein	27g

1 tablespoon avocado oil

1 large red onion, peeled and diced

1 pound 80/20 ground beef

4 ears corn, shucked, stripped of kernels, and cobs saved

½ cup sliced nopalitos (jarred or canned cactus)

2 cups fresh baby spinach

1 (28-ounce) can diced tomatoes, including juice

1 tablespoon chili powder

1 teaspoon salt

1 teaspoon ground cumin

¼ teaspoon cayenne pepper

¼ teaspoon espresso powder

1 small bunch fresh parsley, chopped

1. In a Dutch oven or large pot, heat oil over medium heat. Add red onion and cook 3 minutes or until tender.
2. Add beef, corn kernels, nopalitos, and spinach. Stir-fry 3 minutes or until beef is no longer pink. Add tomatoes and juice, then corn cobs. Add remaining ingredients. Reduce heat to low, cover, and simmer 45 minutes.
3. Remove corn cobs. Stir, ladle chili into individual serving bowls, and serve warm.

Health Benefits of Cactus

Some health benefits of cactus include helping regulate and improve digestion, supporting the immune system, optimizing metabolic activity, improving bone density, promoting good sleep, and reducing inflammation throughout the body. Cactus lends a slightly sweet, melon flavor to your dish.

Chicken Chili Verde

Serves 4

Per Serving

Calories	349
Fat	11g
Sodium	1,847mg
Carbohydrates	28g
Fiber	4g
Sugar	5g
Protein	29g

Poblano Pepper Alternatives

If heat is something you are concerned about, you can always substitute the poblano pepper. If you like a little more kick, go with jalapeños. If you aren't interested in any heat at all, substitute a green bell pepper. Remember, recipes are just guidelines. Learn to cook according to your personal taste buds.

This flavorful and zesty, tangy chili is made with tender chicken simmered in a vibrant green sauce of tomatillos, green chilies, and aromatic herbs. A lighter alternative to traditional chili that is just as comforting, it has a refreshing kick and depth of flavor.

1 tablespoon avocado oil
1 medium white onion, peeled and diced
1 medium poblano pepper, seeded and minced
1 pound boneless, skinless chicken thighs, cut into 1-inch cubes
1 cup Roasted Salsa Verde (Chapter 9)
3 cups chicken broth
1 (15-ounce) can pinto beans, drained and rinsed
1 teaspoon salt
1 teaspoon smoked paprika
1 tablespoon chili powder
1 small bunch fresh parsley, chopped

1. In a Dutch oven or large pot, heat oil over medium heat. Add onion and poblano pepper and cook 3 minutes or until onion is tender. Add chicken. Stir-fry an additional 3 minutes.
2. Stir in remaining ingredients. Reduce heat to low, cover, and simmer 45 minutes.
3. Stir, ladle into individual serving bowls, and serve warm.

Beef Stew

This delicious bowl of goodness traditionally has potatoes. In this recipe, that tuber has been substituted with the humble turnip. The greens of a turnip and of stalks of celery are edible, so don't throw these out. Chop them up and throw them in the stew for a nutritional boost!

Serves 4

Per Serving

Calories	379
Fat	14g
Sodium	1,972mg
Carbohydrates	26g
Fiber	5g
Sugar	11g
Protein	35g

- 1 pound beef stew cubes
- ½ cup chickpea flour
- 2 tablespoons avocado oil, divided
- 1 medium yellow onion, peeled and diced
- 2 medium carrots, scrubbed and diced
- 2 stalks celery, including greens, sliced
- 1 medium turnip, including greens, diced
- 1 cup dry red wine (such as cabernet)
- 4 cloves garlic, peeled and minced
- 1 tablespoon Italian seasoning
- 1 teaspoon minced fresh rosemary
- 4 cups beef broth
- 1 tablespoon Worcestershire sauce
- 1 (6-ounce) can tomato paste
- 1 teaspoon salt
- 1 teaspoon ground black pepper
- 2 bay leaves

1. In a medium bowl, toss beef cubes with flour. Shake off any excess flour. Add 1 tablespoon oil to a large heavy-bottomed pot over medium-high heat. Add beef cubes and cook 3 minutes, turning cubes to brown on all sides. Transfer beef to a plate. Set aside.
2. To the same pot, add remining oil. Add onion, carrots, celery, and turnip. Cook 3 minutes or until onion is tender. Deglaze the pot by adding wine and scraping all the bits from the bottom of the pot. Add garlic, Italian seasoning, rosemary, broth, Worcestershire sauce, tomato paste, salt, black pepper, and bay leaves. Bring to a boil.
3. Reduce heat to low and simmer, uncovered, 30 minutes. Add beef cubes. Cook an additional 30 minutes. Remove and discard bay leaves.
4. Ladle stew into individual serving bowls and serve warm.

Turnips—to Peel or Not to Peel?

Younger, smaller turnips often have tender skins that add earthy flavor and nutrients, making peeling optional. Older or larger turnips, however, tend to have thicker, more bitter skins that are best removed for a smoother taste and texture.

CHAPTER 9

Salads, Dressings, Sauces, and Salsas

Caesar Wedge Salad 204
Southern Egg Salad 204
Watermelon Salad 205
Leftover Rotisserie Chicken Salad 206
Fennel Salad with Grapefruit Caper Vinaigrette 207
BELTA Salad 208
Brussels Sprouts Salad 210
Cocktail Sauce 210
Simple Vinaigrette 211
Kickin' Dijon Mustard Dressing 212
Creamy Caesar Dressing 213
Thousand Island Dressing 214
Homemade Ranch Dressing 215
Mediterranean Cannellini Bean Salad 217
Worcestershire Sauce 218
Russian Dressing 219
Blueberry Ketchup 220
Tzatziki Sauce 221
Cucumber Watermelon Feta Salsa 222
Basil and Grapefruit Pesto 224
Jalapeño and Cilantro Pesto 225
Almond Sage Pesto 226
Roasted Salsa Verde 227
Strawberry Basil Salsa 228
Peach and Sweet Pepper Salsa 228

Caesar Wedge Salad

Serves 4	
Per Serving	
Calories	418
Fat	36g
Sodium	948mg
Carbohydrates	10g
Fiber	2g
Sugar	5g
Protein	10g

This modern twist on the classic Caesar salad features a chilled wedge of iceberg lettuce. Crunchy crushed pork rinds substitute for the croutons traditionally found on a Caesar salad.

1 medium head iceberg lettuce

1 cup Creamy Caesar Dressing (see recipe in this chapter)

¼ cup crushed pork rinds

¼ cup freshly grated Parmesan cheese

2 medium Roma tomatoes, diced

1. Cut iceberg lettuce in half through the stem. Cut in half again, creating 4 wedges.
2. Place a wedge on each of four plates. Drizzle with dressing. Garnish with pork rinds, Parmesan cheese, and tomatoes. Serve.

Southern Egg Salad

Serves 4	
Per Serving	
Calories	255
Fat	19g
Sodium	438mg
Carbohydrates	3g
Fiber	0g
Sugar	1g
Protein	13g

Serve this in a bowl, in a lettuce wrap, or even between two slices of low-carb bread. It is a basic recipe that is steeped in history. It is also simple and delicious.

8 large hard-boiled eggs, peeled and chopped

¼ cup mayonnaise

2 tablespoons dill pickle relish

¼ teaspoon salt

¼ teaspoon ground black pepper

⅛ teaspoon ground nutmeg

In a medium bowl, combine all ingredients. Refrigerate up to 4 days and serve chilled.

Watermelon Salad

This bright summer salad is perfect after a brisk morning stroll. The sweetness of the watermelon and the saltiness of the prosciutto create the base for a well-balanced taste.

Serves 4

Per Serving

Calories	257
Fat	14g
Sodium	232mg
Carbohydrates	19g
Fiber	1g
Sugar	16g
Protein	13g

4 cups diced watermelon

4 ounces prosciutto, torn into pieces

4 ounces crumbled goat cheese

2 tablespoons balsamic vinegar reduction

1⁄4 cup chiffonade fresh basil

1. Add watermelon to individual serving bowls. Distribute prosciutto and goat cheese among bowls.
2. Drizzle balsamic vinegar reduction over bowls. Garnish with basil and serve.

Making Balsamic Vinegar Reduction

Although you can purchase vinegar reduction ready-made in most grocery stores, it is easy to make at home. Add 1 cup balsamic vinegar to a small saucepan. Bring to a boil and simmer, uncovered, 7 minutes or until desired consistency. The sauce will thicken upon cooling. Once cooled, refrigerate until ready to use.

Leftover Rotisserie Chicken Salad

Serves 4

Per Serving

Calories	308
Fat	22g
Sodium	870mg
Carbohydrates	1g
Fiber	0g
Sugar	0g
Protein	22g

If you have some leftover rotisserie chicken, turn it into a tasty lunch for the following day. This salad is delicious in lettuce wraps or between two slices of low-carb bread. Pecan pieces and halved grapes are a nice addition to this recipe.

2 cups chopped chicken
1 stalk celery, diced
½ cup mayonnaise
1 teaspoon yellow mustard
1 tablespoon dill pickle relish
1 teaspoon salt
¼ teaspoon ground black pepper

In a medium bowl, combine all ingredients. Serve immediately. Store refrigerated and covered, up to 5 days.

Fennel Salad with Grapefruit Caper Vinaigrette

This refreshing salad is tossed with juicy grapefruit segments and drizzled in a tangy grapefruit caper vinaigrette. With all that flavor, who needs carb-filled croutons? The crispy capers add a savory crunch, perfectly balancing the salad's bright, citrusy flavors and delicate anise notes.

Serves 4

Per Serving

Calories	135
Fat	10g
Sodium	207mg
Carbohydrates	12g
Fiber	4g
Sugar	7g
Protein	2g

3 tablespoons extra-virgin olive oil, divided

1 tablespoon grapefruit juice

1 tablespoon caper brine

2 tablespoons capers, patted dry

4 cups mixed greens

1 large fennel bulb, cored and thinly sliced

1 tablespoon chopped fennel fronds

2 tablespoons pecan pieces

1 medium grapefruit, cut into 12 segments

1. In a small bowl, whisk together 2 tablespoons oil, grapefruit juice, and caper brine. Set aside.
2. In a small skillet, heat remaining oil over medium-high heat. Add capers and sauté 1–2 minutes until capers are crispy. Transfer capers to a paper towel to drain oil.
3. In a large bowl, add mixed greens and sliced fennel. Toss with juice mixture.
4. Transfer to individual serving bowls. Top with fennel fronds, pecans, grapefruit segments, and fried capers. Serve.

BELTA Salad

Serves 2

Per Serving

Calories	390
Fat	31g
Sodium	665mg
Carbohydrates	12g
Fiber	6g
Sugar	4g
Protein	15g

Don't Join the Avocado Hand Club!

Avocado hand happens when a person uses a knife to remove the pit of an avocado but instead slices through the soft fruit into their hand or fingers. Be careful! Remove the pit by first placing your index and middle finger on either side the pit. Next place your thumb on the peel side of the avocado and push upward to pop the pit out. Remove the avocado flesh using a spoon.

This recipe translates the BLT sammie into salad form and adds a couple of letters to the "B" for "Bacon," "L" for "Lettuce," and "T" for "Tomato": an "E" for "Egg" and an "A" for "Avocado." A tasty meal for two, this dish notches up your childhood lunch memories (minus the bread)!

1⁄4 cup green goddess dressing

3 cups spring greens

3 slices no-sugar-added bacon, cooked and crumbled

2 large hard-boiled eggs, peeled and diced

2 medium Roma tomatoes, diced

1 large avocado, peeled, pitted, and diced

1. In a large bowl, toss dressing with spring greens. Divide between two individual serving bowls.
2. Distribute remaining ingredients between bowls. Serve immediately.

Brussels Sprouts Salad

Serves 4

Per Serving

Calories	287
Fat	20g
Sodium	490mg
Carbohydrates	23g
Fiber	5g
Sugar	13g
Protein	6g

The bitter flavor used to describe Brussels sprouts is masked and balanced in this salad by the tanginess of the vinaigrette, the sweetness of the raisins, and the saltiness of the Parmesan cheese. This is loaded with nutrition, including a touch of protein from the cheese.

1 (10-ounce) bag shaved Brussels sprouts

¼ cup shredded carrots

½ cup Simple Vinaigrette (see recipe in this chapter)

1 medium Granny Smith apple, cored and diced

¼ cup golden raisins

⅓ cup shredded Parmesan cheese

⅓ cup sunflower seeds

In a large bowl, add all ingredients and toss to combine. Serve.

Cocktail Sauce

Yields 1 cup

Per Serving (Serving size: ¼ cup)

Calories	34
Fat	0g
Sodium	767mg
Carbohydrates	7g
Fiber	2g
Sugar	6g
Protein	0g

This sauce has a spicy kick from the horseradish, but if you want extra, don't be afraid to add a little Tabasco. Great with Chilled Shrimp Cocktail (Chapter 3) or Baked Fish Sticks (Chapter 6), this recipe is perfect to make on prep day for a week of seafood!

1 cup no-sugar-added ketchup

2 tablespoons prepared horseradish

1 teaspoon honey

1 teaspoon lemon juice

½ teaspoon Worcestershire sauce

¼ teaspoon garlic powder

In a medium bowl, combine all ingredients. Refrigerate, covered, until ready to use.

Simple Vinaigrette

Making a vinaigrette is so easy to do and avoids those added sugars often included in store-bought versions. You will see these sugars on the ingredient labels listed as “sugar,” “honey,” “cane juice,” and even “fructose.” Bypass them all by making your own!

Yields ½ cup

Per Serving (Serving size: 2 tablespoons)

Calories	166
Fat	18g
Sodium	353mg
Carbohydrates	1g
Fiber	0g
Sugar	9g
Protein	0g

⅓ cup olive oil

2 tablespoons apple cider vinegar

1 tablespoon lemon juice

2 teaspoons Dijon mustard

½ teaspoon salt

¼ teaspoon ground black pepper

In a small bowl, whisk together all ingredients. Refrigerate, covered, until ready to use.

Vinaigrette Variations

There are many variations to a simple vinaigrette. If you want it creamy, add a couple of teaspoons of sour cream or plain Greek yogurt. For a fresh kick, add chopped herbs. Add a little honey or sugar substitute if you want to sweeten it up. Some added horseradish would pair nicely with a steak salad.

Kickin' Dijon Mustard Dressing

Yields 1 cup

Per Serving (Serving size: 1⁄4 cup)

Calories	373
Fat	40g
Sodium	241mg
Carbohydrates	2g
Fiber	1g
Sugar	1g
Protein	0g

Prepared versus Fresh Horseradish

The jarred, prepared horseradish you find in a grocery store is usually mixed with vinegar and salt. If you live on the fresh side of life, pick yourself up a horseradish root in the produce aisle. Trim away the tough skin and grate to your desire. A little goes a long way, so be careful!

This bold, tangy dressing is excellent with a steak salad, as horseradish is a natural friend of beef. It's also low in carbs, making it a smart, flavorful addition to any low-carb meal plan.

3⁄4 cup extra-virgin olive oil

3 tablespoons apple cider vinegar

1 tablespoon balsamic vinegar

1 tablespoon Dijon mustard

2 teaspoons prepared horseradish

1⁄4 teaspoon salt

1⁄4 teaspoon dried Italian seasoning

In a small bowl, combine all ingredients. Taste. Add more salt if necessary. Serve.

Creamy Caesar Dressing

Unlike traditional Caesar dressings, this version does not require raw eggs. Don't worry about losing the classic taste, though, because the signature Caesar flavor is achieved by using anchovy paste, Dijon mustard, and Parmesan cheese.

Yields 1 cup

Per Serving (Serving size: 1/4 cup)

Calories	358
Fat	34g
Sodium	792mg
Carbohydrates	4g
Fiber	0g
Sugar	1g
Protein	6g

3/4 cup mayonnaise
1/4 cup plain full-fat Greek yogurt
2 tablespoons lemon juice
1 teaspoon anchovy paste
2 teaspoons Dijon mustard
1 teaspoon Worcestershire sauce
2 cloves garlic, peeled and minced
1/2 cup freshly grated Parmesan cheese
1/4 teaspoon salt

In a small bowl, combine all ingredients. Refrigerate, covered, until ready to use.

What Is Anchovy Paste?

Anchovy paste is an umami-rich smooth and salty condiment made from ground anchovies and oil. It comes in a tube and can be found in the canned fish and seafood section of most grocery stores. If you cannot find it, you can always use full anchovy fillets. A teaspoon of anchovy paste equals two anchovy fillets.

Thousand Island Dressing

Yields 1 cup

Per Serving (Serving size: 1/4 cup)

Calories	391
Fat	40g
Sodium	766mg
Carbohydrates	4g
Fiber	0g
Sugar	2g
Protein	1g

As with most store-bought versions, bottled Thousand Island dressings have added sugars and preservatives. Use this homemade version on salads, as a special sauce on burgers, or even as a dipping sauce for Baked Onion Rings (Chapter 7).

1 cup mayonnaise

1/4 cup no-sugar-added ketchup

1/4 cup grated sweet yellow onion

2 tablespoons pickle relish

1/2 teaspoon smoked paprika

1 teaspoon white vinegar

1/4 teaspoon salt

1/4 teaspoon garlic powder

In a small bowl, combine all ingredients. Refrigerate, covered, until ready to use.

Homemade Ranch Dressing

Making your own ranch dressing can be achieved in minutes—and the best part is it's all natural and missing the added sugar of store-bought versions. If you want to use this as a dip for vegetables, add less buttermilk for a thicker version.

Yields 1½ cups

Per Serving (Serving size: ¼ cup)

Calories	292
Fat	30g
Sodium	358mg
Carbohydrates	2g
Fiber	0g
Sugar	1g
Protein	1g

1 cup mayonnaise
½ cup sour cream
¼ cup buttermilk
1 teaspoon lemon juice
2 cloves garlic, peeled and minced
2 tablespoons chopped fresh chives
1 teaspoon dried dill
½ teaspoon dried parsley
¼ teaspoon onion powder
¼ teaspoon salt
¼ teaspoon ground black pepper

In a small bowl, combine all ingredients. Refrigerate, covered, until ready to use.

Mediterranean Cannellini Bean Salad

This light, refreshing dish is made with creamy cannellini beans, kalamata olives, red onion, and cucumber all tossed in a zesty lemon-basil dressing. This vibrant salad is perfect as a side or as a healthy, protein-packed meal all on its own.

Serves 4

Per Serving

Calories	268
Fat	11g
Sodium	836mg
Carbohydrates	38g
Fiber	13g
Sugar	4g
Protein	13g

2 tablespoons olive oil

1 tablespoon lemon juice

½ teaspoon salt

¼ teaspoon ground black pepper

2 (15-ounce) cans cannellini beans, drained and rinsed

¼ cup chopped kalamata olives

½ large red onion, peeled and diced

1 medium English cucumber, diced

2 tablespoons minced fresh basil

1 cup halved cherry tomatoes

¼ cup feta cheese

1. In a large bowl, whisk together oil, lemon juice, salt, and black pepper.
2. Add remaining ingredients and toss.
3. Serve immediately or chilled.

You're Not the Boss of Me!

Never be afraid to veer off the path of a recipe. You can simply use it as a guideline. If you don't have cannellini beans and a cucumber, throw in chickpeas and celery or whatever you have on hand. And how about changing things up by using black beans, cilantro, and cotija cheese? Let your imagination go wild!

Worcestershire Sauce

Yields 1 cup

Per Serving (Serving size: 1⁄4 cup)

Calories	38
Fat	0g
Sodium	341mg
Carbohydrates	11g
Fiber	0g
Sugar	3g
Protein	0g

Worcestershire is one of those sauces that lends umami to dishes, and a little goes a long way. Although the store-bought version is convenient, it often contains high-fructose corn syrup and artificial flavors. Make your own for a fresher product and take control of the ingredients you feed your body.

1⁄2 cup apple cider vinegar
1⁄4 cup coconut aminos
1⁄4 cup water
1 tablespoon Swerve brown sugar
1 tablespoon pure maple sugar
1 teaspoon garlic powder
1⁄2 teaspoon ground ginger
1⁄4 teaspoon smoked paprika
1⁄8 teaspoon onion powder
1⁄8 teaspoon ground black pepper
1⁄16 teaspoon ground cinnamon

In a small bowl, combine all ingredients. Refrigerate, covered, until ready to use.

Russian Dressing

Russian dressing is a creamy, tangy blend of mayonnaise, no-sugar-added ketchup, and a hint of horseradish, giving it a slightly bold kick. Finely chopped onions add a little texture, making it a perfect spread for sandwiches, a dip for crisp vegetables, or a dressing atop a steak salad.

Yields 1 cup

Per Serving (Serving size: 1⁄4 cup)

Calories	289
Fat	30g
Sodium	604mg
Carbohydrates	2g
Fiber	0g
Sugar	1g
Protein	1g

3⁄4 cup mayonnaise

1⁄4 cup no-sugar-added ketchup

1 teaspoon prepared horseradish

1⁄2 teaspoon Worcestershire sauce

1⁄4 teaspoon salt

1⁄4 teaspoon smoked paprika

1⁄4 teaspoon ground mustard

1 tablespoon minced white onion

In a small bowl, combine all ingredients. Refrigerate, covered, until ready to use.

Blueberry Ketchup

Yields 1 cup

Per Serving (Serving size: 1⁄4 cup)

Calories	58
Fat	0g
Sodium	73mg
Carbohydrates	27g
Fiber	1g
Sugar	13g
Protein	0g

Does Blueberry Ketchup sound unusual? Don't knock it till you try it! This sweet and tangy condiment offers a unique twist on ketchup, made with antioxidant-rich blueberries instead of tomatoes and added sugars. It's lower in carbs than traditional ketchup thanks to the use of erythritol (a zero-calorie sugar substitute) combined with just a small amount of honey. Plus, it delivers extra vitamins and antioxidants, making it a healthier and flavorful choice for baked fries, burgers, or grilled meats.

1 cup blueberries

1⁄4 medium yellow onion, peeled

1⁄4 cup sugar substitute (like erythritol)

2 tablespoons honey

2 tablespoons apple cider vinegar

Juice of 1 medium lime

1⁄8 teaspoon salt

1⁄4 teaspoon ground ginger

1. Place all ingredients in a food process and pulse until smooth.
2. Serve immediately or refrigerate, covered, up to 2 weeks.

Tzatziki Sauce

Feed your body simpler and more natural foods by making your own sauces—and there is no other sauce as vibrant and bright as tzatziki sauce. Skip the preservatives and serve this fresh with burgers, lamb, or crudités.

Yields 2 cups

Per Serving (Serving size: ¼ cup)

Calories	89
Fat	6g
Sodium	93mg
Carbohydrates	4g
Fiber	0g
Sugar	3g
Protein	5g

½ English cucumber, diced

2 cups plain full-fat Greek yogurt

4 cloves garlic, peeled and minced

2 tablespoons olive oil

1 tablespoon chopped fresh dill

1 teaspoon lemon juice

¼ teaspoon lemon zest

¼ teaspoon salt

¼ teaspoon ground black pepper

In a small bowl, combine all ingredients. Refrigerate, covered, until ready to use.

Cucumber Watermelon Feta Salsa

Yields 3 cups

Per Serving (Serving size: 1⁄4 cup)

Calories	17
Fat	1g
Sodium	223mg
Carbohydrates	2g
Fiber	0g
Sugar	2g
Protein	1g

This salsa is a refreshing, sweet-savory mix of juicy watermelon, fresh tomatoes, crisp cucumber, and tangy feta, tossed with lime juice and fresh herbs. Bursting with bright flavors, this is a delicious topping on low-carb fish or chicken tacos or even as a summer side to any grilled dish. For a nice presentation, garnish this with some extra chopped mint.

1½ cups diced English cucumber

1 cup ½-inch chunks watermelon

2 medium Roma tomatoes, diced

¼ cup diced red onion

1 teaspoon salt

Juice of 1 small lime

1 teaspoon grated lime zest

1 tablespoon chopped fresh mint

1 tablespoon chopped fresh basil

¼ cup crumbled feta cheese

1. In a medium bowl, combine all ingredients.
2. Serve immediately or transfer salsa to a lidded container and refrigerate up to 5 days.

Basil and Grapefruit Pesto

Yields 2 cups

Per Serving (Serving size: 1⁄4 cup)

Calories	161
Fat	16g
Sodium	204mg
Carbohydrates	2g
Fiber	1g
Sugar	0g
Protein	2g

This vibrant pesto combines the herbaceous freshness of basil with the citrusy zing of grapefruit for a refreshing twist on a classic sauce. Rich in healthy fats from pecans and olive oil, it's naturally low in carbs and provides a moderate amount of protein, making it a flavorful, nutrient-dense addition to fish, chicken, or vegetables.

1⁄4 cup pecan pieces
4 cloves garlic, peeled
1 1⁄2 cups fresh basil leaves
1⁄2 cup fresh parsley
1⁄2 teaspoon salt
1⁄4 cup grated Parmesan cheese
1⁄2 cup olive oil
1 tablespoon grapefruit juice
1 teaspoon grapefruit zest

1. In a food processor, add pecans, garlic, basil, parsley, salt, Parmesan cheese, and oil. Pulse until a smooth paste forms.
2. Add grapefruit juice and zest. Pulse to combine.
3. Serve immediately or transfer pesto to a lidded container and refrigerate up to 5 days.

Jalapeño and Cilantro Pesto

This bold pesto blends fresh cilantro, spicy jalapeño, garlic, and lime juice into a zesty, herbaceous sauce with a fiery kick. It makes the perfect topper for your high-protein grilled meats and is also great drizzled over tacos or roasted vegetables.

Yields 2 cups

Per Serving (Serving size: 1⁄4 cup)

Calories	166
Fat	16g
Sodium	62mg
Carbohydrates	2g
Fiber	1g
Sugar	0g
Protein	2g

1⁄4 cup pine nuts

4 cloves garlic, peeled

1 medium jalapeño, seeded and stem removed

1 1⁄2 cups baby spinach

1⁄2 cup chopped fresh cilantro

1⁄4 cup grated Parmesan cheese

1 teaspoon ground cumin

1⁄2 cup olive oil

1 tablespoon lime juice

1 teaspoon lime zest

1. In a food processor, add pine nuts, garlic, jalapeño, spinach, cilantro, Parmesan cheese, cumin, and oil. Pulse until a smooth paste forms.
2. Add lime juice and zest. Pulse to combine.
3. Serve immediately or transfer pesto to a lidded container and refrigerate up to 5 days.

Almond Sage Pesto

Yields 2 cups

Per Serving (Serving size: ¼ cup)

Calories	196
Fat	18g
Sodium	353mg
Carbohydrates	5g
Fiber	2g
Sugar	1g
Protein	3g

The rich, earthy flavor created by combining almonds, fresh sage leaves, garlic, and Parmesan into an aromatic and savory pesto is ideal for roasted vegetables and grilled chicken.

½ cup whole almonds

4 cloves garlic, peeled

1½ cups parsley

½ cup fresh sage leaves

¼ cup grated Parmesan cheese

1 teaspoon salt

¼ teaspoon ground black pepper

½ cup olive oil

1 tablespoon lemon juice

1 teaspoon lemon zest

1. In a food processor, add almonds, garlic, parsley, sage, Parmesan cheese, salt, black pepper, and oil. Pulse until a smooth paste forms.
2. Add lemon juice and zest. Pulse to combine.
3. Serve immediately or transfer pesto to a lidded container and refrigerate up to 5 days.

Roasted Salsa Verde

Tomatillos, a relative of the tomato, are the "verde" contributor to this green goodness. This salsa is delicious served with chicken and fish.

Yields 2 cups

Per Serving (Serving size: ¼ cup)

Calories	26
Fat	0g
Sodium	292mg
Carbohydrates	5g
Fiber	1g
Sugar	3g
Protein	1g

1 pound medium tomatillos, husks removed

2 medium jalapeño peppers, stems removed

1 medium white onion, peeled and cut into 6 wedges

2 cloves garlic, peeled

½ cup chopped fresh cilantro

Juice of 1 small lime

1 teaspoon salt

2 tablespoons water

1. Preheat broiler to high.
2. On a baking sheet lined with parchment paper, scatter tomatillos, jalapeños, onion, and garlic and broil 5 minutes. Rotate pan and broil an additional 5 minutes.
3. Add broiled vegetables to a blender or food processor. Add remaining ingredients and pulse until smooth. Taste and add additional salt and/or water to your preference.
4. Let cool slightly, then transfer to a lidded container and refrigerate at least 30 minutes before serving.

The Spicier Side of Life

If you like your salsas on the spicier side, try substituting serrano peppers for the jalapeños. They are higher on the Scoville scale and will give you the kick you crave!

Strawberry Basil Salsa

Yields 3 cups

Per Serving (Serving size: 1⁄4 cup)

Calories	15
Fat	0g
Sodium	194mg
Carbohydrates	4g
Fiber	1g
Sugar	2g
Protein	0g

Top some baked fish with this salsa and invite the crew over for lunch. This refreshing mix of sweet strawberries, fresh basil, and a splash of lime juice creates a bright and vibrant flavor profile.

2 cups diced strawberries
2 medium Roma tomatoes, diced
1 medium jalapeño pepper, seeded and minced
1⁄2 cup diced red onion
1 teaspoon honey
1 teaspoon salt
Juice of 1 small lime
1 teaspoon lime zest
1⁄4 cup chopped fresh basil

1. In a medium bowl, combine all ingredients.
2. Serve immediately or transfer salsa to a lidded container and refrigerate up to 5 days.

Peach and Sweet Pepper Salsa

Yields 3 cups

Per Serving (Serving size: 1⁄4 cup)

Calories	18
Fat	0g
Sodium	195mg
Carbohydrates	5g
Fiber	1g
Sugar	3g
Protein	1g

This salsa combines juicy peaches with crisp sweet peppers for a sweet and mildly tangy bite. Accented with lemon juice, red onion, and fresh parsley, it's a vibrant topping for pork loins or chops.

2 cups peeled and diced peaches
2 medium Roma tomatoes, diced
6 mini sweet peppers, seeded and minced
1⁄4 cup diced red onion
1 teaspoon Swerve light brown sugar
1 teaspoon salt
Juice of 1 small lemon
1 teaspoon grated lemon zest
1⁄4 cup chopped fresh parsley

1. In a medium bowl, combine all ingredients.
2. Serve immediately or transfer salsa to a lidded container and refrigerate up to 5 days.

CHAPTER 10

Snacks and Desserts

Pimento Cheese–Stuffed Celery 230
Piña Colada–Style Protein Popsicles 230
Spiced Pepitas 231
BLT Cups 233
Spicy Lime Tortilla Chips 234
Sesame Nori Chips 235
Cinnamon-Spiced Apple Chips 236
Portable Cherry Parfaits 237
Grilled Peaches with Whipped Greek Yogurt 238
Chocolate Almond Butter Fudge 240
Peanut Butter Fudge 241
Chocolate Nutty Mixed Clusters 242
Chocolate Mousse 243
Prosciutto-Wrapped Cantaloupe 245
Balsamic Basil Strawberries 246
Peachy Watermelon Popsicles 246
Ginger Plums 247
Peanut and Chocolate–Covered Strawberries 248
Blueberry Protein Smoothie Bowl 249
Strawberry Banana Protein Popsicles 250
Individual Cheesecake Cups 252
Trail Mix 253
Pumpkin Pudding 254

Pimento Cheese–Stuffed Celery

Serves 6

Per Serving

Calories	173
Fat	15g
Sodium	299mg
Carbohydrates	3g
Fiber	1g
Sugar	1g
Protein	5g

For a variation on this snack, you can fill the groove in the celery stalk with a protein-rich nut butter of your choice. Top with raisins for a bit of sweetness!

6 stalks celery, ends trimmed

1 cup Pimento Cheese (Chapter 3)

Using a butter knife, fill celery stalk grooves with Pimento Cheese. Cut into 3-inch sections. Serve.

Piña Colada–Style Protein Popsicles

Serves 6

Per Serving

Calories	159
Fat	4g
Sodium	128mg
Carbohydrates	24g
Fiber	3g
Sugar	16g
Protein	10g

Looking for a tropical treat? These ice pops offer flavor with a little protein to keep you energized and refreshed.

5 cups diced pineapple

1 large ripe banana

½ cup canned coconut milk

Juice of ½ medium lime

¼ cup no-sugar-added vanilla protein powder

¼ teaspoon rum extract

⅛ teaspoon salt

1. In a blender, combine all ingredients and blend until smooth. Pour into six popsicle molds.
2. Freeze overnight. Serve.

Spiced Pepitas

These crunchy, savory pepitas are the perfect high-protein, low-carb snack or salad topper. Tossed with smokey spices and roasted until golden, they're a quick and flavorful way to add texture and nutrition to just about anything, or just enjoy them by the handful!

Serves 6	
Per Serving	
Calories	202
Fat	17g
Sodium	199mg
Carbohydrates	4g
Fiber	2g
Sugar	0g
Protein	10g

½ teaspoon smoked paprika

½ teaspoon salt

½ teaspoon garlic powder

¼ teaspoon chili powder

⅛ teaspoon ground cinnamon

1½ cups pepitas

1 tablespoon avocado oil

1. In a small bowl, combine paprika, salt, garlic powder, chili powder, and cinnamon. Divide mixture in half.
2. In a medium bowl, toss pepitas with oil and half of spice mixture.
3. In a large skillet over medium heat, add pepitas and stir 4 minutes, browning pepitas without burning spices. Remove from heat, toss with remaining half of spices. Serve.

BLT Cups

This lower-carb twist on the classic BLT sandwich will get you excited! Nestled in bacon cups, a delicious blend of cream cheese and Greek yogurt is topped with juicy tomatoes and a fresh crunch of lettuce. Perfect as a quick appetizer or snack, these deliver all the flavor of a BLT in a crunchy handheld bite.

Serves 6

Per Serving

Calories	163
Fat	11g
Sodium	529mg
Carbohydrates	4g
Fiber	0g
Sugar	2g
Protein	10g

½ cup chive and onion cream cheese spread

2 tablespoons plain full-fat Greek yogurt

Juice from ½ small lime

1 large Roma tomato, diced

⅛ teaspoon salt

⅛ teaspoon black pepper

12 slices no-sugar-added bacon, cut into thirds

1½ cups shredded lettuce

1. In a medium bowl, whip together cream cheese, yogurt, and lime juice. Refrigerate, covered, until ready to use.
2. Place tomato in a small bowl and season with salt and black pepper. Toss with your hands to coat. Set aside.
3. Preheat oven to 400°F. Flip a 6-cup muffin tin upside down over an ungreased baking sheet. Coat muffin tin with nonstick cooking spray.
4. Drape 3 bacon strips in a row over one of the upturned muffin cups, overlapping slightly. Perpendicular to the original strips, drape 3 more strips in a row, overlapping slightly. The cup should be covered completely. Repeat with remaining upturned cups. Bake 25 minutes.
5. Remove bacon cups from the oven and transfer upright to a paper towel–lined plate. Once bacon cups cool, spoon cream cheese mixture in each.
6. Garnish with shredded lettuce and tomato dices. Serve.

Spicy Lime Tortilla Chips

Serves 4

Per Serving

Calories	135
Fat	9g
Sodium	571mg
Carbohydrates	20g
Fiber	13g
Sugar	0g
Protein	5g

What Is Nutritional Yeast?

Often found in vegan dishes, nutritional yeast is a deactivated yeast used as a seasoning. Known for its cheesy, nutty flavor and rich nutritional profile, it's a popular plant-based source of B vitamins, including B_{12}. It is easily found in the baking aisle at most grocers.

If you are craving something salty and snacky, these chips are an easy way to enjoy a crunchy bite with your favorite dip.

½ teaspoon salt

⅛ teaspoon cayenne pepper

⅛ teaspoon smoked paprika

2 teaspoons nutritional yeast

4 (8-inch) low-carb flour tortillas

2 tablespoons avocado oil

Juice from 1 large lime

1. Preheat oven to 350°F.
2. In a small bowl, combine salt, cayenne pepper, paprika, and nutritional yeast.
3. Cut each tortilla into 8 triangular sections. Brush oil over tortillas and place on an ungreased baking sheet. Brush tortillas with lime juice. Sprinkle with seasoning mix.
4. Bake 7 minutes. Let rest 10 minutes to harden. Serve.

Sesame Nori Chips

Naturally low in carbohydrates and high in umami, this nutrient-rich snack delivers a big punch of flavor!

Serves 6

Per Serving

Calories	41
Fat	4g
Sodium	101mg
Carbohydrates	1g
Fiber	1g
Sugar	0g
Protein	1g

2 tablespoons sesame oil

2 tablespoons avocado oil

5 nori sheets

¼ teaspoon salt

2 teaspoons white sesame seeds

1. Preheat oven to 325°F. Line a baking sheet with parchment paper.
2. In a small bowl, combine oils. Brush some on the parchment paper. Place nori sheets on oiled parchment paper. Brush tops of nori with oils. Sprinkle with salt and sesame seeds.
3. Bake 5 minutes. Remove from oven and let cool 5 minutes. Cut each sheet into 6 squares and serve.

What Is Umami?

Umami is known as the fifth taste, along with sweet, salty, sour, and bitter. It is described as a savory or meaty flavor lending to a more satisfying bite of food. It is found in foods like mushrooms, soy sauce, aged cheese, and nori.

Cinnamon-Spiced Apple Chips

Serves 8	
Per Serving	
Calories	39
Fat	0g
Sodium	36mg
Carbohydrates	11g
Fiber	1g
Sugar	8g
Protein	0g

Naturally gluten-free and free of refined sugar, these apple chips are great for snacking or adding to your charcuterie board or as a quick boost on the hiking trail.

1 teaspoon ground cinnamon

⅛ teaspoon ground nutmeg

⅛ teaspoon salt

4 medium gala apples, cored and sliced into ⅛-inch rounds

1. Preheat oven to 200°F. Line two baking sheets with parchment paper.
2. In a small bowl, combine cinnamon, nutmeg, and salt.
3. Place apple rounds on baking sheets. Sprinkle apples with seasoning.
4. Place baking sheets on different racks in oven. Bake 1 hour. Switch baking sheets on the racks. Bake an additional hour. If you want crisper chips, bake 30 additional minutes.
5. Let cool completely before serving.

Portable Cherry Parfaits

These are a great dessert to make on your meal prep day. Each parfait is easy to grab and add to your lunch box when you are craving something sweet. Get creative with different fruits or berries and different flavors of pudding to change up this recipe each week.

2 cups cherries, pitted and halved

¼ cup water

2 tablespoons Swerve granulated sugar

2 teaspoons lemon juice

½ teaspoon vanilla extract

1 (1.34-ounce) package sugar-free lemon pudding, prepared per package instructions

½ cup pecan pieces

1 cup sugar-free whipped topping

1. In a medium saucepan, add cherries, water, sugar, lemon juice, and vanilla extract. Bring to a boil. Reduce heat to low and simmer 5 minutes. Strain through a sieve and let cool completely.
2. Distribute prepared pudding among six (4-ounce) Mason jars, then distribute pecans among jars. Add cooled cherry coulis to each jar and top with whipped topping. Place lids on jars.
3. Refrigerate and serve chilled.

Serves 6

Per Serving

Calories	135
Fat	7g
Sodium	244mg
Carbohydrates	22g
Fiber	2g
Sugar	7g
Protein	1g

Toasting Nuts

Although raw nuts are delicious, toasting them adds to their texture, nuttiness, and crispness. When cooking nuts already chopped, cook them in a small dry skillet over medium heat 3 minutes. When cooking whole or halved, cook 5 minutes in skillet and then chop. No oil is required. Keep the nuts moving in the skillet so as not to burn.

Grilled Peaches with Whipped Greek Yogurt

Serves 4

Per Serving

Calories	205
Fat	10g
Sodium	42mg
Carbohydrates	22g
Fiber	3g
Sugar	20g
Protein	8g

If you've never grilled fruit, you are missing out! The heat brings the fruit's sweetness alive and takes its flavor profile up another level. Try this with nectarines, plums, and pineapple too. Grilled fruit is low in calories because it relies on the natural sweetness of the fruit with little added sugar. The Greek yogurt adds not only a creamy element but protein as well.

1 cup plain full-fat Greek yogurt

2 teaspoons fresh orange juice

1 teaspoon grated orange zest

½ teaspoon vanilla extract

1 tablespoon honey

1 tablespoon salted butter

4 medium ripe peaches, sliced in half, pits removed

¼ cup chopped walnuts

1. With an electric mixer, whip together yogurt, orange juice, orange zest, vanilla extract, and honey until fluffy.
2. On a grilling pan, melt butter over medium-high heat. Coat the pan with the melted butter. Add peaches, cut side down, and grill 5 minutes.
3. Transfer peaches to individual serving bowls cut side up and top with whipped yogurt mixture and walnuts. Serve.

Chocolate Almond Butter Fudge

Serves 24

Per Serving

Calories	147
Fat	14g
Sodium	25mg
Carbohydrates	16g
Fiber	4g
Sugar	1g
Protein	2g

This creamy indulgence uses low-carb ingredients to fit into your high-protein, low-carb lifestyle. The addition of almond butter adds a touch of protein, and the crushed almonds give the fudge a little textural crunch for some guilt-free snacking. Unsweetened coconut flakes are another yummy topper!

1 (9-ounce) bag no-sugar-added milk chocolate chips (like Lily's)

½ cup almond butter

½ cup unsalted butter, cut into 5 sections

2 ounces cream cheese, room temperature

¾ cup heavy cream

2 teaspoons vanilla extract

1⁄16 teaspoon salt

1 cup Swerve granulated sugar

¼ cup crushed salted almonds

1. In a large microwave-safe bowl, add chocolate chips, almond butter, unsalted butter, cream cheese, heavy cream, and vanilla. Microwave in 30-second intervals, stirring between intervals until smooth. Stir in salt and sugar.
2. Pour mixture into an 8" × 8" baking dish lined with parchment paper. Scatter crushed almonds over top.
3. Refrigerate 4 hours or until set. Cut into twenty-four squares. Serve chilled.

Peanut Butter Fudge

This rich and creamy peanut butter fudge combines no-sugar-added white chocolate chips, cream cheese, and peanut butter for a silky-smooth texture. With its sprinkle of crushed salted peanuts, each bite delivers the perfect balance of sweet and salty. This lower-carb version of fudge will let you indulge your sweet tooth without spiking your blood sugar.

Serves 24

Per Serving

Calories	110
Fat	14g
Sodium	30mg
Carbohydrates	16g
Fiber	3g
Sugar	1g
Protein	2g

1 (9-ounce) bag no-sugar-added white chocolate chips (like Lily's)

½ cup no-sugar-added peanut butter

½ cup unsalted butter, cut into 5 sections

2 ounces cream cheese, room temperature

¾ cup heavy cream

2 teaspoons vanilla extract

1⁄16 teaspoon salt

1 cup Swerve granulated sugar

¼ cup crushed salted peanuts

1. In a large microwave-safe bowl, add white chocolate chips, peanut butter, unsalted butter, cream cheese, heavy cream, and vanilla. Microwave in 30-second intervals, stirring between intervals until smooth. Stir in salt and sugar.
2. Pour mixture into an 8" × 8" baking dish lined with parchment paper. Scatter crushed peanuts over top.
3. Refrigerate 4 hours or until set. Cut into twenty-four squares. Serve chilled.

Chocolate Nutty Mixed Clusters

Serves 6

Per Serving

Calories	393
Fat	34g
Sodium	73mg
Carbohydrates	73g
Fiber	15g
Sugar	5g
Protein	9g

Let your imagination go wild when preparing this recipe. The pecans, peanuts, and sunflower seeds can be substituted for whatever nuts and seeds your taste buds enjoy or are in your pantry. Also, there are several flavors of no-sugar-added chips to experiment with.

1 (9-ounce) bag no-sugar-added milk chocolate chips (like Lily's)

2 tablespoons coconut oil

½ cup pecan halves

½ cup salted peanuts

¼ cup raisins

¼ cup salted sunflower seeds

¼ cup unsweetened coconut

1. Line a baking sheet with parchment paper.
2. In a medium microwave-safe bowl, add chocolate chips and coconut oil. Microwave in 30-second intervals, stirring between each interval until smooth. Do not over-microwave.
3. Add remaining ingredients to melted chocolate. Place tablespoonfuls of chocolate mixture on parchment paper. Refrigerate 1 hour before serving.

Chocolate Mousse

This creamy delicacy is sure to end your day right. Made with cream cheese, heavy cream, and cocoa powder, it offers a satisfying dose of fat and protein while keeping carbs moderate. The banana and honey add natural sweetness, so it's not ultra-low carb, but it's still a more balanced dessert option than the typical confection, especially when enjoyed with fresh sliced strawberries.

Serves 4

Per Serving

Calories	406
Fat	34g
Sodium	324mg
Carbohydrates	17g
Fiber	3g
Sugar	11g
Protein	5g

6 ounces cream cheese, softened

1 cup heavy cream

2 teaspoons vanilla extract

1 large ripe banana

1 tablespoon honey

4 tablespoons cocoa powder

1⁄4 teaspoon salt

1. In the bowl of a stand mixer, beat cream cheese on high until fluffy.
2. Slowly beat in cream on medium until incorporated and then add remaining ingredients until all are blended.
3. Transfer mixture to individual serving bowls. Serve immediately or cover and refrigerate for 1 hour or up to 3 days.

Prosciutto-Wrapped Cantaloupe

This simple yet elegant appetizer pairs sweet, juicy cantaloupe with salty prosciutto for a perfect balance of flavors. This no-cook dish is ideal for warm-weather gatherings or as a light, refreshing starter.

Serves 2

Per Serving

Calories	252
Fat	17g
Sodium	248mg
Carbohydrates	13g
Fiber	1g
Sugar	10g
Protein	13g

½ medium cantaloupe, seeded, peeled, and sliced into fourths

4 ounces (about 8 slices) prosciutto

2 teaspoons extra virgin olive oil

1 tablespoon sliced fresh basil

⅛ teaspoon ground black pepper

1. Wrap each slice of cantaloupe in 1 ounce prosciutto.
2. Drizzle with oil and top with basil and black pepper. Serve immediately.

Balsamic Basil Strawberries

Serves 4	
Per Serving	
Calories	40
Fat	0g
Sodium	73mg
Carbohydrates	10g
Fiber	2g
Sugar	7g
Protein	1g

This lovely and easy summer surprise is delicious on its own but is also amazing topped with sugar-free whipped cream or ice cream.

1 pound fresh strawberries, hulled and quartered

¼ cup freshly squeezed orange juice

1 teaspoon orange zest

1 teaspoon balsamic vinegar

1 teaspoon white vinegar

⅛ teaspoon salt

1 tablespoon chopped fresh basil

In a medium bowl, add all ingredients. Stir to combine. Refrigerate, covered, until ready to serve.

Peachy Watermelon Popsicles

Serves 6	
Per Serving	
Calories	90
Fat	1g
Sodium	56mg
Carbohydrates	19g
Fiber	2g
Sugar	16g
Protein	3g

Simply delicious! Because these cold summer treats do not contain refined sugar, make sure your fruit is ripe to take advantage of its natural sweetness. The Greek yogurt not only lends creaminess but a hint of protein as well.

5 cups diced watermelon

3 medium peaches, peeled, pitted, and diced

Juice from 1 medium orange

½ cup unsweetened full-fat plain Greek yogurt

⅛ teaspoon salt

1. In a blender, combine all ingredients and blend until smooth. Pour into six popsicle molds.
2. Freeze overnight. Serve.

Ginger Plums

Sometimes a simple dish can be the most elegant. In this recipe, the natural sweetness of the plums is enhanced by the fresh ginger and the sugar substitute. These plums pair beautifully with a scoop of low-carb ice cream or a dollop of whipped cream.

Serves 2

Per Serving

Calories	62
Fat	0g
Sodium	0mg
Carbohydrates	28g
Fiber	2g
Sugar	13g
Protein	0g

4 medium plums, pitted and halved

1 tablespoon grated fresh ginger

2 tablespoons Swerve brown sugar

1. Preheat oven to 400°F. Line a baking sheet with parchment paper.
2. Place plum halves on baking sheet. Top plum halves with ginger and sugar.
3. Bake 15 minutes. Serve warm.

Peeling Ginger Hack

Because of all the knobs and grooves of ginger root, using a knife to peel it can be tricky. Simply use the edge of a small spoon to gently scrape away the skin. Not only is this safer, but you'll also retain more of the ginger than by cutting or using a peeler.

Peanut and Chocolate-Covered Strawberries

Serves 4

Per Serving

Calories	337
Fat	28g
Sodium	29mg
Carbohydrates	49g
Fiber	21g
Sugar	5g
Protein	8g

The natural sweetness and freshness of strawberries are only enhanced with a dip in milk chocolate. The salty peanuts lend some protein and a welcome textural crunch. Enjoy these as a dessert or as a treat for guests.

¼ cup chopped salted peanuts

1 (9-ounce) bag no-sugar-added milk chocolate chips (like Lily's)

1 tablespoon coconut oil

¾ pound fresh strawberries, stems removed

1. Add peanuts to a small bowl. Place a piece of parchment paper on a cutting board.
2. In a medium microwave-safe bowl, add chocolate chips and coconut oil. Microwave in 30-second intervals, stirring between each interval, until smooth.
3. Making sure it's fully dry, dip a strawberry halfway in melted chocolate, then dip in peanuts. Place each dipped strawberry on parchment paper.
4. Refrigerate 30 minutes and serve.

Blueberry Protein Smoothie Bowl

A naturally sweet, creamy dessert, this smoothie bowl is loaded with protein, blending silken tofu, peanut butter, and Greek yogurt for a satisfying texture. Topped with fresh blueberries, crunchy pecans, and flaxseed meal, it's a nourishing treat chock-full of nutrition.

Serves 4

Per Serving

Calories	288
Fat	18g
Sodium	88mg
Carbohydrates	20g
Fiber	6g
Sugar	11g
Protein	14g

1 (12.3-ounce) package silken tofu, drained

2 cups blueberries, divided

1⁄3 cup plain full-fat Greek yogurt

1⁄4 cup peanut butter

1 teaspoon vanilla extract

1⁄2 cup unsweetened vanilla almond milk

1⁄4 cup pecan pieces

1⁄4 cup flaxseed meal

1. In a food processor, pulse tofu, 1 cup blueberries, yogurt, peanut butter, vanilla, and almond milk until smooth. Add additional milk if necessary to achieve your desired consistency.
2. Divide among individual serving bowls and garnish with remaining blueberries, pecan pieces, and flaxseed meal. Serve.

Strawberry Banana Protein Popsicles

Serves 6

Per Serving

Calories	89
Fat	1g
Sodium	129mg
Carbohydrates	12g
Fiber	2g
Sugar	7g
Protein	10g

These refreshing frozen treats are made with strawberries, Greek yogurt, a ripe banana, and a scoop of protein powder for a nutritious boost. Perfect for post-workout recovery or a healthy summer snack, they are naturally sweet and creamy with no added sugar.

1 pound strawberries, stems removed

1 large ripe banana, peeled

Juice from 1 medium orange

¼ cup plain full-fat Greek yogurt

¼ cup no-sugar-added vanilla protein powder

¼ teaspoon vanilla extract

⅛ teaspoon salt

1. In a blender, combine all ingredients and blend until smooth. Pour into six popsicle molds.
2. Freeze overnight. Serve.

Individual Cheesecake Cups

Serves 8

Per Serving

Calories	439
Fat	36g
Sodium	385mg
Carbohydrates	16g
Fiber	2g
Sugar	8g
Protein	7g

This low-carb, guilt-free, and portioned dessert is rich and creamy. Replacing a traditional heavy crust, the toasted pecans lend some crunchy texture along with a bit of sweetness from the honey.

1½ cups pecan pieces

2 tablespoons honey

6 tablespoons unsalted butter, melted

12 ounces cream cheese, softened

1 (1-ounce) package instant sugar-free cheesecake pudding mix

1 cup whole milk

1 cup evaporated milk

½ teaspoon vanilla extract

⅛ teaspoon salt

1. In a small bowl, combine pecans, honey, and butter. Add mixture to a medium skillet over medium heat. Toss continuously 2–3 minutes until nuts are browned. Remove from heat and transfer nuts to a small shallow plate. Set aside.
2. In a blender, blend cream cheese until smooth. Slowly blend in remaining ingredients until smooth. Transfer to individual serving bowls. Refrigerate, covered, until set, about 1 hour.
3. Serve chilled and garnished with pecan mixture.

Trail Mix

Free of added refined sugar, this crunchy and nourishing snack is perfect for on-the-go energy on a hiking trail or even as a crunchy topping for Greek yogurt. You may also want to add it with a little vanilla almond milk to a small bowl if you are craving cereal.

Yields 2 cups

Per Serving (Serving size: 1⁄4 cup)

Calories	262
Fat	21g
Sodium	74mg
Carbohydrates	20g
Fiber	7g
Sugar	6g
Protein	7g

1⁄2 cup almond slivers

1⁄2 cup cashew pieces

1⁄2 cup pepitas

1⁄2 cup unsweetened coconut flakes

2 tablespoons coconut oil, melted

2 tablespoons honey

1⁄2 teaspoon vanilla extract

1⁄4 teaspoon salt

1⁄4 teaspoon ground cinnamon

1⁄2 cup no-sugar-added chocolate chips

1. Preheat oven to 350°F. Line a baking sheet with parchment paper.
2. In a medium bowl, combine all ingredients except chocolate chips. Spread mixture on baking sheet. Bake 15 minutes. Remove from oven and let cool completely.
3. Toss in chocolate chips. Enjoy immediately or store mixture in an airtight container.

Pumpkin Pudding

Serves 6

Per Serving

Calories	93
Fat	4g
Sodium	350mg
Carbohydrates	12g
Fiber	1g
Sugar	2g
Protein	3g

This creamy, sweet dessert, made with pumpkin purée, warm spices, and a package of sugar-free vanilla pudding, creates a wholesome and cozy treat that's rich in flavor and perfect for fall or any time you crave something comforting.

1 cup canned pumpkin purée

1 (1-ounce) package instant sugar-free vanilla pudding mix

1 cup unsweetened almond milk

1 cup evaporated milk

1 teaspoon pumpkin pie spice

¼ teaspoon salt

1. In a blender, blend all ingredients until smooth.
2. Pour into six small lidded containers. Refrigerate until set, about 1 hour. Serve. Can be refrigerated up to 3 days.

Weekly Meal Plans

Please note, these meal plans focus on the recipes in this book, but in order to meet your individual macronutrient needs, you may need to incorporate other whole foods (fruits, vegetables, whole grains, and dairy). Some of these types of foods have been added to these meal plans for balance. Also, these meal plans are not low in sodium. If you are following a low-sodium diet for health reasons, adjust the salt in the recipes to meet your needs.

WEEK 1

	Breakfast	Lunch
Day 1	■ Mediterranean Egg Bites (3) Chapter 2 ■ Breakfast Sausage Patties Chapter 2 ■ 1 cup blueberries	■ BBQ Shrimp Chapter 6 ■ Tex-Mex Zucchini Boats (2) Chapter 7 ■ ½ cup no-added-sugar apple sauce
Day 2	■ Mediterranean Egg Bites (3) Chapter 2 ■ Breakfast Sausage Patties Chapter 2 ■ 1 cup blueberries	■ BBQ Shrimp Chapter 6 ■ Tex-Mex Zucchini Boats (2) Chapter 7 ■ ½ cup no-added-sugar apple sauce
Day 3	■ Mediterranean Egg Bites (3) Chapter 2 ■ Breakfast Sausage Patties Chapter 2 ■ 1 cup blueberries	■ Salmon Patties with Sriracha Lime Crema Chapter 6 ■ 1 baked sweet potato ■ ½ cup no-added-sugar apple sauce
Day 4	■ Loaded Yogurt Bowls Chapter 2 ■ 1 cup blueberries	■ Sloppy Turkey Janes Chapter 4 ■ Low-carb bun ■ 1 apple
Day 5	■ Loaded Yogurt Bowls Chapter 2 ■ 1 cup blueberries	■ Sloppy Turkey Janes Chapter 4 ■ Low-carb bun ■ 1 apple
Day 6	■ Morning Hash Bowls Chapter 2 ■ 1 cup melon	■ Pork Egg Roll Bowl Chapter 5
Day 7	■ Morning Hash Bowls Chapter 2 ■ 1 cup melon	■ Mediterranean Cannellini Bean Salad Chapter 9 ■ 1 packet lemon pepper tuna ■ ½ cup nonfat Greek Yogurt

WEEK 1

	Dinner	Snack/Dessert
Day 1	■ Sweet Pepper Steak Chapter 5 ■ Lower-Carb Garlic Mashed Potatoes Chapter 7	■ Chocolate Banana Protein Smoothie Chapter 2 ■ Portable Cherry Parfaits Chapter 10
Day 2	■ Sweet Pepper Steak Chapter 5 ■ Lower-Carb Garlic Mashed Potatoes Chapter 7	■ Cinnamon-Spiced Apple Chips Chapter 10 ■ Portable Cherry Parfaits Chapter 10
Day 3	■ Chicken Thighs, Brussels Sprouts, and Pears Chapter 4	■ Cinnamon-Spiced Apple Chips Chapter 10 ■ Chocolate Banana Protein Smoothie Chapter 2 ■ ½ cup nonfat Greek yogurt
Day 4	■ Chicken Thighs, Brussels Sprouts, and Pears Chapter 4	■ Cinnamon-Spiced Apple Chips Chapter 10 ■ Prosciutto-Wrapped Cantaloupe Chapter 10
Day 5	■ Pork Egg Roll Bowl Chapter 5	■ Caramelized Onion Dip Chapter 3 ■ Carrot sticks (1 cup) ■ 2 hard-boiled eggs
Day 6	■ Pan-Seared Salmon Chapter 6 ■ Cast Iron Brussels Sprouts Chapter 7 ■ 1 baked sweet potato	■ Caramelized Onion Dip Chapter 3 ■ Carrot sticks (1 cup) ■ Grilled Peaches with Whipped Greek Yogurt Chapter 10
Day 7	■ Beef and Broccoli Chapter 5 ■ ½ cup brown rice	■ Grilled Peaches with Whipped Greek Yogurt Chapter 10 ■ Chocolate Banana Protein Smoothie Chapter 2

WEEK 2

	Breakfast	Lunch
Day 1	■ Creamy Ricotta Chive Scrambled Eggs **Chapter 2** ■ Breakfast Sausage Patties **Chapter 2** ■ Whole-grain sandwich thin	■ Portobello Pizzas **Chapter 7** ■ 2 cups mixed greens with 2 tablespoons Homemade Ranch Dressing **Chapter 9**
Day 2	■ Creamy Ricotta Chive Scrambled Eggs **Chapter 2** ■ Breakfast Sausage Patties **Chapter 2** ■ Whole-grain sandwich thin	■ Baked Fish Sticks **Chapter 6** ■ Brussels Sprouts Salad **Chapter 9**
Day 3	■ Huevos Rancheros with Salsa Verde **Chapter 2** ■ 1 cup strawberries ■ Whole-grain sandwich thin	■ Fish Tacos **Chapter 6**
Day 4	■ Huevos Rancheros with Salsa Verde **Chapter 2** ■ 1 cup strawberries	■ Tex-Mex Turkey Chili **Chapter 8** ■ 1 sweet potato
Day 5	■ Cinnamon Berry and Cottage Cheese Toast **Chapter 2** ■ 2 hard-boiled eggs ■ 1 cup nonfat Greek yogurt	■ Tex-Mex Turkey Chili **Chapter 8** ■ 1 sweet potato
Day 6	■ Cubano Egg Cups **Chapter 2** ■ Blistered Tomatoes **Chapter 7** ■ Whole-grain sandwich thin	■ Chicken Lettuce Wraps (2) **Chapter 4** ■ 1 cup shelled edamame
Day 7	■ Cubano Egg Cups **Chapter 2** ■ Blistered Tomatoes **Chapter 7** ■ Whole-grain sandwich thin	■ Chicken Lettuce Wraps (2) **Chapter 4** ■ 1 cup shelled edamame

WEEK 2

	Dinner	Snack/Dessert
Day 1	■ No-Noodle Beef Stroganoff **Chapter 5** ■ 1 sweet potato	■ Tropical Protein Smoothie **Chapter 2** ■ 1 cup nonfat Greek yogurt ■ 1 cup strawberries
Day 2	■ No-Noodle Beef Stroganoff **Chapter 5** ■ 1 sweet potato	■ Tropical Protein Smoothie **Chapter 2** ■ ½ cup nonfat Greek yogurt ■ 1 cup strawberries
Day 3	■ Chicken Meatballs with Pesto **Chapter 4** ■ 1 cup spaghetti squash ■ Oven-Roasted Parmesan Broccoli **Chapter 7**	■ Strawberry Banana Protein Popsicles **Chapter 10** ■ 1 cup nonfat Greek yogurt ■ 1 cup blueberries
Day 4	■ Chicken Meatballs with Pesto **Chapter 4** ■ 1 cup spaghetti squash ■ Oven-Roasted Parmesan Broccoli **Chapter 7**	■ Peach and Sweet Pepper Salsa **Chapter 9** ■ 1 ounce tortilla chips ■ Strawberry Banana Protein Popsicles **Chapter 10** ■ 1 cup nonfat Greek yogurt
Day 5	■ Protein Lentil Bowls **Chapter 7**	■ Peach and Sweet Pepper Salsa **Chapter 9** ■ 1 ounce tortilla chips ■ Strawberry Banana Protein Popsicles **Chapter 10**
Day 6	■ Curried Coconut Shrimp **Chapter 6** ■ ½ cup brown rice	■ Balsamic Basil Strawberries **Chapter 10** ■ ½ cup no-sugar-added vanilla ice cream ■ Chocolate Banana Protein Smoothie **Chapter 2**
Day 7	■ Curried Coconut Shrimp **Chapter 6** ■ ½ cup brown rice	■ Balsamic Basil Strawberries **Chapter 10** ■ ½ cup no-sugar-added vanilla ice cream ■ Chocolate Banana Protein Smoothie **Chapter 2**

WEEK 3

	Breakfast	Lunch
Day 1	■ Caprese Avocado Toast Chapter 2 ■ 1 cup Greek yogurt ■ 1 cup strawberries	■ Southern Egg Salad Chapter 9 ■ Whole-grain sandwich thin ■ Caesar Wedge Salad Chapter 9
Day 2	■ Caprese Avocado Toast Chapter 2 ■ 1 cup Greek yogurt ■ 1 cup strawberries	■ Southern Egg Salad Chapter 9 ■ Whole-grain sandwich thin ■ Caesar Wedge Salad Chapter 9
Day 3	■ Loaded Yogurt Bowls Chapter 2	■ Veggie Sammie Chapter 7 ■ Air Fryer Avocado Fries Chapter 7
Day 4	■ Five-Ingredient Fluffy Pancakes Chapter 2 ■ Breakfast Sausage Patties Chapter 2 ■ 1 cup melon	■ Veggie Sammie Chapter 7 ■ Air Fryer Avocado Fries Chapter 7
Day 5	■ Five-Ingredient Fluffy Pancakes Chapter 2 ■ Breakfast Sausage Patties Chapter 2 ■ 1 cup melon	■ Watermelon Salad Chapter 9 ■ Baked Pimento Cheese Jalapeño Poppers Chapter 3
Day 6	■ Bacon, Cheddar, and Arugula Frittata Chapter 2 ■ 1 cup melon ■ 1 cup oatmeal	■ Cheeseburger Soup Chapter 8 ■ 2 cups mixed greens with 2 tablespoons Homemade Ranch Dressing Chapter 9
Day 7	■ Bacon, Cheddar, and Arugula Frittata Chapter 2 ■ 1 cup melon ■ 1 cup oatmeal	■ Cheeseburger Soup Chapter 8 ■ 1 sweet potato

WEEK 3

	Dinner	Snack/Dessert
Day 1	■ Chicken Piccata Chapter 4 ■ Dilled Roasted Carrots Chapter 7 ■ ½ cup brown rice	■ Chocolate Banana Protein Smoothie Chapter 2 ■ 1 tablespoon no-sugar-added peanut butter ■ 1 celery stalk
Day 2	■ Chicken Piccata Chapter 4 ■ Dilled Roasted Carrots Chapter 7 ■ ½ cup brown rice	■ Chocolate Banana Protein Smoothie Chapter 2 ■ 1 tablespoon no-sugar-added peanut butter ■ 1 celery stalk
Day 3	■ Beef Soft Tacos Chapter 5 ■ ½ cup refried black beans	■ Pimento Cheese Stuffed Celery Chapter 10 ■ Apple with 1 tablespoon no-sugar-added peanut butter
Day 4	■ Beef Soft Tacos Chapter 5 ■ ½ cup refried black beans	■ Pimento Cheese–Stuffed Celery Chapter 10 ■ Apple with 1 tablespoon no-sugar-added peanut butter
Day 5	■ Chicken Gyro Bowls Chapter 4 ■ 1 cup tricolor quinoa	■ ½ serving Trail Mix Chapter 10 ■ ½ cup nonfat Greek yogurt ■ 1 cup strawberries
Day 6	■ Caper and Lemon Butter Halibut Chapter 6 ■ Oven-Roasted Parmesan Broccoli Chapter 7 ■ 1 sweet potato	■ ½ serving Trail Mix Chapter 10 ■ 1 cup nonfat Greek yogurt ■ 1 cup strawberries
Day 7	■ Pan-seared Salmon Chapter 6 ■ Loaded Mashed Cauliflower Chapter 7 ■ Roasted Radishes Chapter 7	■ Blueberry Protein Smoothie Bowl Chapter 10 ■ 1 cup nonfat Greek yogurt ■ 1 cup strawberries

WEEK 4

	Breakfast	Lunch
Day 1	■ Cheddar Cheesy Scrambled Eggs Chapter 2 ■ Breakfast Sausage Patties Chapter 2 ■ 1 cup blueberries	■ Bean Burger Patties Chapter 7 ■ Whole-grain sandwich thin ■ Grilled Green Tomatoes Chapter 7
Day 2	■ Cheddar Cheesy Scrambled Eggs Chapter 2 ■ Breakfast Sausage Patties Chapter 2 ■ 1 cup blueberries	■ Bean Burger Patties Chapter 7 ■ Whole-grain sandwich thin ■ Grilled Green Tomatoes Chapter 7
Day 3	■ Goat Cheese Avocado Toast Chapter 2 ■ 2 hard-boiled eggs	■ Thai Burger Patties with Quick-Pickled Vegetables Chapter 5 ■ Whole-grain sandwich thin ■ 2 cups mixed greens with 2 tablespoons Homemade Ranch Dressing Chapter 9
Day 4	■ Goat Cheese Avocado Toast Chapter 2 ■ 2 hard-boiled eggs	■ Thai Burger Patties with Quick-Pickled Vegetables Chapter 5 ■ Whole-grain sandwich thin ■ 2 cups mixed greens with 2 tablespoons Homemade Ranch Dressing Chapter 9
Day 5	■ South-of-the-Border Breakfast Burritos Chapter 2 ■ 1 cup strawberries	■ Enchilada Turkey Pie Chapter 4 ■ 1 cup melon
Day 6	■ South-of-the-Border Breakfast Burritos Chapter 2 ■ 1 cup strawberries	■ Enchilada Turkey Pie Chapter 4 ■ 1 cup melon
Day 7	■ Smoked Salmon and Cottage Cheese Toast Chapter 2 ■ 1 cup melon	■ Navy Bean Soup Chapter 8 ■ 2 cups mixed greens with 2 tablespoons Homemade Ranch Dressing Chapter 9

WEEK 4

	Dinner	Snack/Dessert
Day 1	■ Roasted Pork Tenderloin, 2 servings Chapter 5 ■ Summer Squash Casserole Chapter 7	■ Peachy Watermelon Popsicles Chapter 10 ■ Pumpkin Pudding Chapter 10
Day 2	■ Roasted Pork Tenderloin, 2 servings Chapter 5 ■ Summer Squash Casserole Chapter 7	■ Peachy Watermelon Popsicles Chapter 10 ■ Pumpkin Pudding Chapter 10
Day 3	■ Mini Meatloaves Chapter 5 ■ Loaded Mashed Cauliflower Chapter 7	■ Roasted Red Pepper Hummus Chapter 3 ■ ½ cup carrots and ½ cup cucumbers ■ 1 ounce pita chips ■ 1 cup nonfat Greek yogurt
Day 4	■ Mini Meatloaves Chapter 5 ■ Loaded Mashed Cauliflower Chapter 7	■ Roasted Red Pepper Hummus Chapter 3 ■ ½ cup carrots and ½ cup cucumbers ■ 1 ounce pita chips ■ 1 cup nonfat Greek yogurt
Day 5	■ Cast Iron Cod and Ratatouille-Style Vegetables Chapter 6 ■ ½ cup brown rice	■ Roasted Red Pepper Hummus Chapter 3 ■ ½ cup carrots and ½ cup cucumbers ■ 1 ounce pita chips ■ 1 cup nonfat Greek yogurt
Day 6	■ Chicken Parmesan Chapter 4 ■ 1 cup spaghetti squash	■ Individual Cheesecake Cups Chapter 10 ■ 1 cup nonfat Greek yogurt
Day 7	■ Chicken Parmesan Chapter 4 ■ 1 cup spaghetti squash	■ Individual Cheesecake Cups Chapter 10 ■ 1 cup nonfat Greek yogurt

Index

Note: Page numbers in **bold** indicate recipe category lists.

A

Aging/mature adults, this diet and, 17
Air Fryer Avocado Fries, 154
Almond Sage Pesto, 226
Anchovy paste, about, 213
Appetizers and dips, **47**–70
Apple chips, cinnamon-spiced, 236
Artichoke Heart Hummus, 66
Avocados
  about: cutting safely, 208
  Air Fryer Avocado Fries, 154
  BELTA Salad, 208–9
  Caprese Avocado Toast, 40
  Goat Cheese Avocado Toast, 37

B

Bacon
  about: added sugar in, 24
  Bacon, Cheddar, and Arugula Frittata, 26
  Bacon Cauli Fauxtato Soup, 178
  BELTA Salad, 208–9
  BLT Cups, 233
  Mediterranean Egg Bites, 24
  Onion and Bacon Jam, 62
Baked Baby Back Pork Ribs, 120–21
Baked Chicken Wings, 50
Baked Crab Cakes, 150
Baked Fish Sticks, 127
Baked Onion Rings, 166
Baked Pimento Cheese Jalapeño Poppers, 57
Baked Tilapia, 139
Balsamic Basil Strawberries, 246
Bananas
  Chocolate Banana Protein Smoothie, 43
  Strawberry Banana Protein Popsicles, 250–51
Basil and Grapefruit Pesto, 224
BBQ Shrimp, 137
Beans and other legumes
  about: chickpea flour, 154
  Artichoke Heart Hummus, 66
  Bean Burger Patties, 167
  Black Bean Hummus, 65
  Chorizo and Black Bean Soup, 179
  Enchilada Turkey Pie, 91
  Huevos Rancheros with Salsa Verde, 35
  Mediterranean Cannellini Bean Salad, 217
  Navy Bean Soup, 187
  Protein Lentil Bowls, 169
  Roasted Red Pepper Hummus, 61
  Tex-Mex Zucchini Boats, 168
  Veggie Sammie, 156–57
Beef
  about: slicing against the grain, 106
  Beef and Broccoli, 103
  Beef Soft Tacos, 107
  Beef Stew, 201
  Bunless Beef Sliders, 98
  Cheeseburger Soup, 185
  Cowboy Sirloin Steaks, 104
  Cowgirl Cactus Chili, 199
  Homemade Beef Broth, 177
  Margarita Flank Steak, 100
  Mini Meatloaves, 99
  Mozzarella-Stuffed Meatballs, 111

No-Noodle Beef Stroganoff, 106
Philly Cheesesteak Bowls, 108–9
Reuben Frittata, 27
Sloppy Joe Casserole, 110
Steak Bites with Blue Cheese Crumbles, 70
Stuffed Beefsteak Tomatoes, 112
Sweet Pepper Steak, 105
Taco Meatzza, 101
BELTA Salad, 208–9
Berries
Balsamic Basil Strawberries, 246
Blueberry Ketchup, 220
Blueberry Protein Smoothie Bowl, 249
Cinnamon Berry and Cottage Cheese Toast, 42
Loaded Yogurt Bowls, 43
Peanut and Chocolate–Covered Strawberries, 248
Strawberry Banana Protein Popsicles, 250–51
Strawberry Basil Salsa, 228
Black Bean Hummus, 65
Blistered Tomatoes, 170
BLT Cups, 233
Blueberries. *See* Berries
Blue Cheese Dip, 57
Bowls
Blueberry Protein Smoothie Bowl, 249
Chicken Gyro Bowls, 75
Loaded Yogurt Bowls, 43
Morning Hash Bowls, 34
Philly Cheesesteak Bowls, 108–9
Pork Egg Roll Bowl, 116
Protein Lentil Bowls, 169
Breakfast and brunch, **23**–46
Breakfast Denver Burritos, 38
Breakfast Sausage Patties, 33
Broccoli
Beef and Broccoli, 103
Creamy Broccoli Soup, 181
Oven-Roasted Parmesan Broccoli, 159
Sheet Pan Drumsticks and Vegetables, 77
Bruschetta Chicken Tenders, 80
Brussels sprouts
Brussels Sprouts Salad, 210
Cast Iron Brussels Sprouts, 155
Chicken Thighs, Brussels Sprouts, and Pears, 73
Buffalo Chicken Deviled Eggs, 49
Buffalo Chicken Dip, 56
Bunless Beef Sliders, 98
Burgers, 115, 123, 167. *See also* Cheeseburger Soup
Butter Shrimp, 133

C

Cabbage
Spicy Cabbage and Turkey Smoked Sausage, 92–93
Sweet and Tangy Braised Red Cabbage, 163
Caesar Wedge Salad, 204
Cantaloupe, prosciutto-wrapped, 245
Caper and Lemon Butter Halibut, 143
Caprese Avocado Toast, 40
Caramelized Onion Dip, 54
Carrots. *See also* Quick-Pickled Vegetables
about: carrot greens uses, 160
Carrot and Ginger Miso Soup, 192
Dilled Roasted Carrots, 160
Cast Iron Brussels Sprouts, 155
Cast Iron Cod and Ratatouille-Style Vegetables, 129
Cast iron skillets, about, 155
Cauliflower
Bacon Cauli Fauxtato Soup, 178
Loaded Mashed Cauliflower, 152
Roasted Halloumi and Cauliflower, 158
Vegetable Soup, 191
Cheddar Cheesy Scrambled Eggs, 32
Cheese. *See also* Appetizers and dips
about: Halloumi, 158; Swiss cheese slices, 28
eggs with (*See* Eggs)
Enchilada Turkey Pie, 91
Goat Cheese Avocado Toast, 37
Individual Cheesecake Cups, 252
Mozzarella-Stuffed Meatballs, 111
Mushroom and Swiss–Stuffed Pork Chops, 119

Cheese—*continued*
Pimento Cheese–Stuffed Celery, 230
Roasted Halloumi and Cauliflower, 158
sandwiches with (*See* Sandwiches, wraps, and modified sandwiches)
toast with (*See* Toast)
Cheeseburger Soup, 185
Cherry parfaits, portable, 237
Chicken, main dishes, **71**–96. *See also* Poultry, other
Chicken Chili Verde, 200
Chicken Gyro Bowls, 75
Chicken Lettuce Wraps, 74
Chicken Meatballs with Pesto, 89
Chicken Parmesan, 81
Chicken Piccata, 79
Chicken Thighs, Brussels Sprouts, and Pears, 73
Chicken Thighs with Creamy Dijon Sauce, 85
Chickpeas. *See* Beans and other legumes
Chili, 194, 199
Chilled Shrimp Cocktail, 68–69
Chocolate
Chocolate Almond Butter Fudge, 240
Chocolate Banana Protein Smoothie, 43
Chocolate Mousse, 243
Chocolate Nutty Mixed Clusters, 242
Peanut and Chocolate–Covered Strawberries, 248
Trail Mix, 253
Chorizo. *See* Sausage
Cilantro, about, 179. *See also* Jalapeño and Cilantro Pesto
Cinnamon Berry and Cottage Cheese Toast, 42
Cinnamon-Spiced Apple Chips, 236
Classic Breakfast Casserole, 30
Cocktail Sauce, 210
Coconut milk, in can vs. carton, 84
Collard greens, in Southern Potlikker Soup, 186
Corn
Corn Bread Topping, 110
Cowgirl Cactus Chili, 199
Tex-Mex Zucchini Boats, 168
Vegetable Soup, 191
Cornish Hens, 96
Cowboy Sirloin Steaks, 104
Cowgirl Cactus Chili, 199
Crab Bisque, 197
Creamy Broccoli Soup, 181
Creamy Caesar Dressing, 213
Creamy Dill Chicken Bites, 86
Creamy Hearts of Palm Linguini with Shrimp, 140–41
Creamy Ricotta Chive Scrambled Eggs, 31
Croutons, homemade, 183
Crusted Chili Lime Cod, 126
Cubano Egg Cups, 25
Cucumbers
Cucumber Watermelon Feta Salsa, 222–23
Raw Oysters with Cucumber Shallot Relish, 67
Curried Coconut Shrimp, 132
Curried Deviled Eggs, 48

D

Desserts and snacks, **229**–54
Diabetes, this diet and, 17
Dilled Roasted Carrots, 160
Dips and appetizers, **47**–70
Duck and Butternut Squash Stew, 190

E

Easy Chicken Casserole, 87
Easy French Onion Soup, 188–89
Egg roll bowl, port, 116
Eggs
about: flax egg substitute, 167
Bacon, Cheddar, and Arugula Frittata, 26
Breakfast Denver Burritos, 38
Buffalo Chicken Deviled Eggs, 49
Cheddar Cheesy Scrambled Eggs, 32
Classic Breakfast Casserole, 30
Creamy Ricotta Chive Scrambled Eggs, 31
Cubano Egg Cups, 25
Curried Deviled Eggs, 48
Ham, Swiss, and Roasted Red Pepper Frittata, 28–29
Hard-Boiled Quail Eggs, 46
Huevos Rancheros with Salsa Verde, 35
Mediterranean Egg Bites, 24

Reuben Frittata, 27
Southern Egg Salad, 204
South-of-the-Border Breakfast Burritos, 39
Enchilada Turkey Pie, 91

F

Fajita-Style Chicken Kebabs, 82–83
Fennel Salad with Grapefruit Caper Vinaigrette, 207
Fiber, 18
Fire-Roasted Tomato Soup, 183
Fish and seafood, main dishes, **125**–50
Fish and seafood, other
about: debearding mussels, 144; differences in crabmeat, 150; finding shucked oysters, 67
Chilled Shrimp Cocktail, 68–69
Crab Bisque, 197
Fish Stew, 195
Manhattan Clam Chowder, 198
Raw Oysters with Cucumber Shallot Relish, 67
Smoked Salmon and Cottage Cheese Toast, 41
Spinach and Crab Dip, 58
Fish Tacos, 147
Five-Ingredient Fluffy Pancakes, 44–45
Flax egg, about, 167
Fond, about, 190
Food choices and preparation, 19–21
Food labels, reading, 18–19
Fruity Caprese Skewers, 53

G

Garlic Basil Frenched Rack of Lamb, 122
Ginger miso soup, carrots and, 192
Ginger Plums, 247
Goat Cheese Avocado Toast, 37
Grapefruit, in Basil and Grapefruit Pesto, 224
Grilled Green Tomatoes, 171
Grilled Peaches with Whipped Greek Yogurt, 238–39

H

Ham
Breakfast Denver Burritos, 38
Ham, Swiss, and Roasted Red Pepper Frittata, 28–29
Prosciutto-Wrapped Cantaloupe, 245
Southern Potlikker Soup, 186
Hard-Boiled Quail Eggs, 46
Hasselback Chicken Breasts, 78
Heart health, this diet and, 17–18
High-protein, low-carb living
about: overview and perspective on, 1, 13; this book and, 11
benefits of, rationale for, 15–18
carbohydrates, sugars and, 14, 18–19
fats and, 14
fiber and, 18–19
food choices and preparation, 19–21
food labels (reading) and, 18–19
groups who can benefit from, 16
kitchen tools and utensils, 21–22
macronutrients and, 14
power of, 16
proteins and, 14
strictly high-protein or low-carb diets vs., 15–16
Homemade Beef Broth, 177
Homemade Chicken Broth, 176
Homemade Ranch Dressing, 215
Honey Mustard Dipping Sauce, 64
Horseradish, preparing fresh, 212
Huevos Rancheros with Salsa Verde, 35
Hummus, 61, 65, 66

I

Individual Cheesecake Cups, 252
Inflammation, this diet and, 17
Island Chicken Thighs, 84

J

Jalapeño and Cilantro Pesto, 225

K

Kebabs and skewers, 53, 82–83, 137
Ketchup, blueberry, 220
Kickin' Dijon Mustard Dressing, 212
Kitchen tools and utensils, 21–22

L

Lamb, garlic basil French rack of, 122
Lamb Burgers, 123
Leftover Rotisserie Chicken Salad, 206
Lentil bowls, protein, 169
Lettuce wraps, 74, 145, 206
Loaded Mashed Cauliflower, 152
Loaded Yogurt Bowls, 43
Lobster Lettuce Wraps, 145
Lower-Carb Garlic Mashed Potatoes, 153

M

Manhattan Clam Chowder, 198
Margarita Flank Steak, 100
Marinated Turkey Legs, 95
Mayonnaise labels, about, 64
Meal plans, weekly, 255–63
Meatballs, 89, 111
Meat thermometer, about, 104
Mediterranean Cannellini Bean Salad, 217
Mediterranean Egg Bites, 24
Menopause, this diet and, 17
Mexican Mussels, 144
Mini Cheese Balls, 59
Mini Meatloaves, 99
Miso soup, 192, 193
Morning Hash Bowls, 34
Mozzarella-Stuffed Meatballs, 111
Muscle, building, 16
Mushrooms
  Mushroom and Swiss–Stuffed Pork Chops, 119
  Portobello Pizzas, 172–73
  Slow Cooker Mushrooms, 174
  Three-Ingredient Stuffed Mushrooms, 51
  Wild Mushroom Soup, 182

N

Navy Bean Soup, 187
No-Noodle Beef Stroganoff, 106
Nori chips, sesame, 235
Nutritional yeast, about, 234
Nutrition facts, reading food labels and, 18–19
Nuts
  about: toasting, 237
  Almond Sage Pesto, 226
  Peanut and Chocolate–Covered Strawberries, 248
  Peanut Butter Fudge, 241
  Thai Peanut "Noodles" with Shrimp, 136
  Trail Mix, 253

O

Old Bay Seasoning, copycat, 149
Olives, kalamata vs. black, 75
Onions
  about: caramelized onions, 62
  Baked Onion Rings, 166
  Caramelized Onion Dip, 54
  Easy French Onion Soup, 188–89
  Onion and Bacon Jam, 62
  Quick-Pickled Red Onions, 174
Oven Pulled Pork, 113
Oven-Roasted Parmesan Broccoli, 159

P

Pancakes, five-ingredient, 44–45
Pan-Seared Salmon, 135
Parchment paper pockets, 138
Parmesan Flounder, 133
Pasta
  about: spaghetti squash noodles, 81
  Creamy Hearts of Palm Linguini with Shrimp, 140–41
  Thai Peanut "Noodles" with Shrimp, 136
Peach and Sweet Pepper Salsa, 228
Peaches
  Fruity Caprese Skewers, 53
  Grilled Peaches with Whipped Greek Yogurt, 238–39
  Peach and Sweet Pepper Salsa, 228
  Peachy Watermelon Popsicles, 246
Peanut Butter Fudge, 241
Pears, chicken thighs, brussels sprouts, and, 73
Pecan-Crusted Barramundi, 142
Pepitas, spiced, 231
Peppers
  about: bell pepper rainbow, 38; poblano alternatives, 200
  Baked Pimento Cheese Jalapeño Poppers, 57
  Ham, Swiss, and Roasted Red Pepper Frittata, 28–29

Jalapeño and Cilantro Pesto, 225
Peach and Sweet Pepper Salsa, 228
Roasted Red Pepper Hummus, 61
Sweet Pepper Steak, 105
Veggie Sammie, 156–57
Perimenopause, this diet and, 17
Philly Cheesesteak Bowls, 108–9
Pimento Cheese, 63
Pimento Cheese–Stuffed Celery, 230
Piña Colada–Style Protein Popsicles, 230
Pizza, Taco Meatzza, 101
Pizzas, portobello, 172–73
Plums, ginger, 247
Plums, skillet pork chops with, 118
Pork
about: pork rinds, 126
Baked Baby Back Pork Ribs, 120–21
Mushroom and Swiss–Stuffed Pork Chops, 119
Oven Pulled Pork, 113
Pork Egg Roll Bowl, 116
Roasted Pork Tenderloin, 117
Skillet Pork Chops with Plums, 118
Thai Burger Patties with Quick-Pickled Vegetables, 115
Portable Cherry Parfaits, 237
Portobello Pizzas, 172–73
Potatoes
Bacon Cauli Fauxtato Soup, 178
Lower-Carb Garlic Mashed Potatoes, 153
Poultry, main dishes, **71**–96
Poultry, other. *See also* Turkey
about: giblets, 72
Baked Chicken Wings, 50
Buffalo Chicken Deviled Eggs, 49
Buffalo Chicken Dip, 56
Chicken Chili Verde, 200
Homemade Chicken Broth, 176
Leftover Rotisserie Chicken Salad, 206
Thai Coconut Chicken Soup, 184
Preparation, food choices and, 19–21
Prosciutto-Wrapped Cantaloupe, 245
Protein Lentil Bowls, 169
Pumpkin Pudding, 254

Q

Quick Miso Soup, 193
Quick-Pickled Red Onions, 174
Quick-Pickled Vegetables, 115
Quick Turkey Stir-Fry, 94

R

Radishes, roasted, 161
Raw Oysters with Cucumber Shallot Relish, 67
Reuben Frittata, 27
Roasted Halloumi and Cauliflower, 158
Roasted Pork Tenderloin, 117
Roasted Radishes, 161
Roasted Red Pepper Hummus, 61
Roasted Salsa Verde, 227
Russian Dressing, 219

S

Salads, dressings, sauces, and salsas, **203**–28
Salmon Patties with Sriracha Lime Crema, 130
Sandwiches, wraps, and modified sandwiches. *See also* Burgers
Beef Soft Tacos, 107
Breakfast Denver Burritos, 38
Bunless Beef Sliders, 98
Chicken Lettuce Wraps, 74
Fish Tacos, 147
Leftover Rotisserie Chicken Salad (in lettuce wraps), 206
Lobster Lettuce Wraps, 145
Philly Cheesesteak Bowls, 108–9
South-of-the-Border Breakfast Burritos, 39
Veggie Sammie, 156–57
Zucchini Tacos, 165
Sausage
Breakfast Sausage Patties, 33
Chorizo and Black Bean Soup, 179
Classic Breakfast Casserole, 30
Morning Hash Bowls, 34
South-of-the-Border Breakfast Burritos, 39

Sausage—*continued*
Spicy Cabbage and Turkey Smoked Sausage, 92–93
Three-Ingredient Stuffed Mushrooms, 51
Sea Bass in Parchment (en Papillote), 138
Seafood. *See* Fish and seafood *entries*
Sesame Nori Chips, 235
Sheet Pan Drumsticks and Vegetables, 77
Simple Vinaigrette, 211
Skewers and kebabs, 53, 82–83, 137
Skillet Pork Chops with Plums, 118
Sloppy Joe Casserole, 110
Sloppy Turkey Janes, 90
Slow Cooker Mushrooms, 174
Smoked Salmon and Cottage Cheese Toast, 41
Smoothies
Blueberry Protein Smoothie Bowl, 249
Chocolate Banana Protein Smoothie, 43
Tropical Protein Smoothie, 46
Snacks and desserts, **229**–54
Snow Crab Legs with Chili Mustard Butter, 131
Soups, stews, and chilis, **175**–201
Southern Egg Salad, 204
Southern Potlikker Soup, 186
South-of-the-Border Breakfast Burritos, 39
Spiced Pepitas, 231
Spicy Cabbage and Turkey Smoked Sausage, 92–93
Spicy Lime Tortilla Chips, 234
Spinach and Crab Dip, 58
Spinach Tots, 55
Squash
Cast Iron Cod and Ratatouille-Style Vegetables, 129
Duck and Butternut Squash Stew, 190
Summer Squash Casserole, 162
Tex-Mex Zucchini Boats, 168
Zucchini Tacos, 165
Steak Bites with Blue Cheese Crumbles, 70
Steamed Littleneck Clams, 148
Steamed Lobster Tails, 149
Strawberries. *See* Berries
Strawberry Basil Salsa, 228
Stuffed Beefsteak Tomatoes, 112
Sugar and carbs, food labels and, 18–19
Sugars, carbs and, 14, 18–19
Summer Squash Casserole, 162
Sweet Pepper Steak, 105
Sweet potatoes, in Morning Hash Bowls, 34

T

Taco Meatzza, 101
Tacos, 107, 147, 165
Tex-Mex Turkey Chili, 194
Tex-Mex Zucchini Boats, 168
Thai Burger Patties with Quick-Pickled Vegetables, 115
Thai Coconut Chicken Soup, 184
Thai Peanut "Noodles" with Shrimp, 136
Thousand Island Dressing, 214
Three-Ingredient Stuffed Mushrooms, 51
Toast
Caprese Avocado Toast, 40
Cinnamon Berry and Cottage Cheese Toast, 42
Goat Cheese Avocado Toast, 37
Smoked Salmon and Cottage Cheese Toast, 41
Tofu
Blueberry Protein Smoothie Bowl, 249
Quick Miso Soup, 193
Tomatoes
about: dressing up green tomatoes, 171
BELTA Salad, 208–9
Blistered Tomatoes, 170
BLT Cups, 233
Fire-Roasted Tomato Soup, 183
Grilled Green Tomatoes, 171
Stuffed Beefsteak Tomatoes, 112
Trail Mix, 253
Tropical Protein Smoothie, 46
Turkey
main dishes, 90–95
Tex-Mex Turkey Chili, 194
Thai Burger Patties with Quick-Pickled Vegetables, 115
Turnips, in Beef Stew, 201
Tzatziki Sauce, 221

U

Umami, about, 235

V

Vegetables. *See also specific vegetables*
- Cast Iron Cod and Ratatouille-Style Vegetables, 129
- Thai Burger Patties with Quick-Pickled Vegetables, 115
- Vegetable Soup, 191
- Veggie Sammie, 156–57

Vegetarian, mains and sides, **151**–74
Veggie Sammie, 156–57

W

Watermelon Salad, 205. *See also* Cucumber Watermelon Feta Salsa; Peachy Watermelon Popsicles
Weight loss medications, this diet and, 16–17
Whole Roasted Chicken, 72
Wild Mushroom Soup, 182
Worcestershire Sauce, 218

Y

Yogurt
- Blueberry Protein Smoothie Bowl, 249
- Grilled Peaches with Whipped Greek Yogurt, 238–39
- Loaded Yogurt Bowls, 43

Z

Zucchini. *See* Squash